SURVIVAL
SKILLS

FOR THE
AFRICAN-AMERICAN
WOMAN

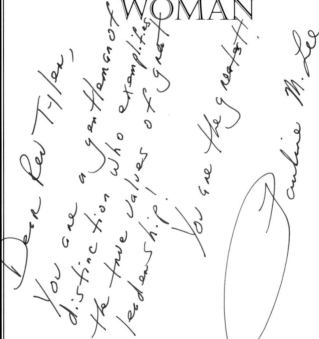

Dear Rev T-1/04,
You are a gentleman of
distinction who exemplifies
the true values of great
leadership! You are the greatest!!

Aurelius M. Lee

Edited by Linda Ellis Eastman

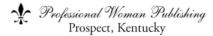

Professional Woman Publishing
Prospect, Kentucky

Published by:
Professional Woman Publishing
Post Office Box 333
Prospect, KY 40059
(502) 228-0906
http://www.prowoman.net

Please contact the publisher for quantity discounts.

ISBN 13: 978-0-9791153-5-6
ISBN 10: 0-9791153-4-5

Library of Congress Cataloging-In-Publication Data

Typography by:
Sential Design, LLC — www.sentialdesign.com

Printed in the United States of America

Dedicated to Myrna Marshall Brame for living a life of courage, strength, kindness, and amazing grace.

TABLE OF CONTENTS

TABLE OF CONTENTS
-CONTINUED-

TABLE OF CONTENTS
–CONTINUED–

ABOUT THE AUTHOR

LINDA EASTMAN

Linda Ellis Eastman is President and CEO of The Professional Woman Network (PWN), an International Training and Consulting Organization on Women's Issues. She has designed seminars which have been presented in China, the former Soviet Union, South Africa, the Phillipines, and attended by individuals in the United States from such firms as McDonalds, USA Today, Siemens-Westinghouse, the Pentagon, the Department of Defense, and the United States Department of Education.

An expert on women's issues, Ms. Eastman has certified and trained over one thousand women to start consulting/seminar businesses originating from such countries as Pakistan, the Ukraine, Antigua, Canada, Mexico, Zimbabwe, Nigeria, Bermuda, Jamaica, Costa Rica, England, South Africa, Malaysia, and Kenya. Founded in 1982 by Linda Ellis Eastman, The Professional Woman Network is committed to educating women on a global basis regarding, self-esteem, confidence building, stress management, and emotional, mental, spiritual and physical wellness.

Ms. Eastman has been featured in USA Today and listed in Who's Who of American Women, as well as Who's Who of International Leaders. In addition to women's issues, Ms. Eastman speaks internationally regarding the importance of human respect as it relates to race, color, culture, age, and gender. She will be facilitating an international conference where speakers and participants from many nations will be able to discuss issues that are unique to women on a global basis.

Linda Ellis Eastman is also founder of The Professional Woman Speakers Bureau and The Professional Woman Coaching Institute. Ms. Eastman has dedicated her businesses to increasing the self-esteem and personal dignity of women and youth around the world.

Contact
The Professional Woman Network
P.O. Box 333
Prospect, KY 40059
(502) 566-9900
lindaeastman@prodigy.net
www.prowoman.net
www.protrain.net

INTRODUCTION

Linda Ellis Eastman

This book is written for the African-American woman who wishes increased self-esteem, healthier relationships, and joyful living.

African-American women are soul-searchers. Therefore, I have asked twenty four women of color and one African-American male to share information that will help today's Black woman walk on her emotional, mental, physical and spiritual path with courage and support.

The authors who have written this book *Survival Skills for the African-American Woman*, are consultants, personal coaches, ministers, and persons of deep faith. They share with you step-by-strategies for understanding yourself and others, and encourage you, the reader, to be personally involved in each chapter.

I wish you such a blessed journey on your walk in life. May you always be true to yourself while embracing your glorious Afrocentricity. May this book become a ready resource for you when you need support, guidance, and encouraging words.

Linda Ellis Eastman

SURVIVAL SKILLS

SKILLS

FOR THE
AFRICAN-AMERICAN
WOMAN

ABOUT THE AUTHOR

PAULINE M. LEE

Pauline M. Lee is Chief Executive Officer of Etiquette Works, Inc. Additionally, she serves as Director of Program Management Analysis with the Los Angeles County Metropolitan Transportation Authority (Metro) and has over 25 years experience in the work place. She has gained extensive knowledge and experience in management, effective customer service, public speaking skills, training, and life issues through these positions. She is an expert in international protocol, business etiquette, and young adult/ youth manners. She is known for her seminars, keynote presentations, personal, and professional development seminars. Ms. Lee is committed to helping individuals acquire the polish, productivity, and professionalism necessary to thrive and excel in this ever-changing, super information highway, high technology, global economy. Pauline provides her listeners with interactive training and the tools needed to remove the business etiquette obstacles and minimize the irritations that make doing business a pain rather than a pleasure.

Ms. Lee is certified as an International Protocol and Business Etiquette Specialist by The Protocol School of Washington; has a Masters Degree in Public Administration and a Bachelor of Science Degree in Business Administration. Ms. Lee is a member of The International Society of Protocol and Etiquette Professionals (ISPEP), National Speakers Association (NSA), and Toastmasters International (ATM-G). She is active in her community and serves on the Board of Directors of the Joseph L. Holmes Community Center and the Wattstar Theatre Project and is the Director of Women's Ministry at Double Rock Baptist Church.

Pauline is an informative, energetic, and humorous presenter. It is her desire that all people exhibit confidence, project intelligence, speak clearly, concisely and eloquently while achieving the greatness they deserve. She is dedicated to providing workshops and seminars that increase self-esteem, personal empowerment, leadership and overall confidence in the dining room, classroom and the Boardroom.

Contact:
ETIQUETTE WORKS, INC.
6709 LaTijera Boulevard #550
Los Angeles, California 90045
(323) 253-1908
etiquetteworks@sbcglobal.net
www.protrain.net

ONE

DIGNITY AND GRACE: ETIQUETTE FOR TODAY'S WOMAN

By Pauline M. Lee

Y ou have the experience, skills, and perhaps the education, but you did not get the callback for a second interview or were not invited to the reception. Why? What went wrong? You have pondered it time after time and still can't figure it out.

Could it be that you have forgotten the importance of good manners? Could it be a negative and sarcastic attitude instead of maintaining dignity and grace? Could it be that society has taken the "business" out of "business casual" and you have become comfortable with poor appearance and/or inappropriate dress for the occasion? Could it be that you have forgotten the common courtesies, such as "please" and "thank you"?

Etiquette in today's society plays an important part in presenting oneself as professional, productive, and polished. Because "etiquette" comes from the Louis XIV era, we often think it has no place in today's society. In the past, when we heard the word "etiquette" we would think "snobbish", "stuck up", or "elitist". We would think "boring set of structured rules" for table manners. Now is an opportunity for a paradigm shift and to expand our thinking. Proper etiquette allows us to present ourselves with dignity and grace at all times. Proper etiquette enables us to express ourselves while remaining flexible enough to value the beliefs and opinions of others. Etiquette is not limited to table manners. It is reflected in our everyday living. It is about treating others the way we would like to be treated. We say, "Good morning." That's dignity and grace. We say, "Excuse me," and turn our cell phones to off or to vibrate while out to dinner or at the movies. We send "thank you notes" to acknowledge thoughtfulness. That's dignity and grace. Etiquette is about civility—the very foundation of what our strong mothers and grandmothers taught us. Using proper etiquette shows respect for the people you are with. Without etiquette, we would not speak with confidence and assurance. Without etiquette, our assertiveness would be mistaken for aggressiveness or arrogance. Without etiquette, we would talk with our mouths full of food or drive with road rage.

First impressions are lasting impressions, and you never get a second chance to make a good first impression. Etiquette is about presenting yourself with the kind of polish that shows you can be taken seriously. Therefore, introductions are important in making a good first impression. Remember that the person you may have just met could become a client, business acquaintance, even a new friend. There are several things to keep in mind when making an introduction:

- A firm handshake. (Nothing is worse than a limp, wet, clammy or bone-crushing handshake.)

- Make eye contact. (When meeting new people, be mindful of them; look them in the eye; be personable.)

- Smile. (It has been said that people who smile are perceived to be more intelligent than those who don't. Smiling is infectious and once given, is usually returned.)

- Say your name to them, and once they tell you their name, say their name back to them. (If you find yourself in a group and do not know everyone, introduce yourself.)

- Rise to the occasion. Everyone (even women) should stand to greet new people entering the room or office. (When in the office, come around your desk to greet someone.)

- When someone accompanies the contact person, always acknowledge his or her guest by making eye contact, saying hello, or quickly introducing yourself, if appropriate. (Make it a point to greet individuals who accompany people and you will make a difference.)

- Keep business cards in perfect condition. Carry them in a business-card holder to prevent creasing and smudging. Ask, "May I give you my card?" Conversely, don't just turn around and say to someone, "Can I have your card?" Instead, ask: "Is there a way to get in touch with you?" Or: "May I contact you? What is the best way?" When receiving a business card, look at it intently before placing it into your wallet or purse. Taking a moment to look at the card demonstrates your interest. Avoid writing on the face of the card in the presence of the giver, because it could be offensive.

- Introductions in the business world tend to be based on power and authority or rank. People of "lesser" authority are introduced to people of "greater" authority. (Example: "Mr./Ms. "higher rank," allow me to introduce Mr./Ms. "lesser rank.") When introducing your spouse or the guest with you, put the name before the description. (Example: "This is George, my husband.")

- Don't always bring business right into the conversation when meeting someone by immediately asking, "And what do you do?" It may make people feel uncomfortable, and may be perceived as trying to determine if the person is worth your time. Instead, begin with general conversation such as, "Did you see today's headlines?" or "What is a good movie/video to see?"

Presenting oneself as polished is a matter of practice. In today's global high technology and fast food society, we often forget to practice good manners.

Dining Etiquette

Nothing will ruin a good first impression faster than bad, messy table manners. Regardless of whether we are having lunch with a prospective employer or dinner at the office holiday party, our manners speak volumes about us. Your inability to handle yourself as is expected could be expensive – no one will tell you the "real" reason you didn't get the job, promotion, or invitation to the social engagement. Fair or not, others equate bad manners with incompetence and a lack of discipline. Before you sit down, go to each person at the table to whom you have not met beforehand. Extend your hand and introduce yourself. Say hello to guests you already know by name. You will make a memorable impression by taking the time to greet each guest personally. The following tips will allow you to focus on your agenda and enjoy the participants, rather than stressing yourself by watching to see what others are doing and how they do it:

- Napkin Use – You want to put your napkin on your lap soon after sitting down at the table (but follow your host's/hostesses' lead). The napkin remains on your lap throughout the entire meal, and should be used to gently blot your mouth when needed. If you must leave the table during the meal, place your napkin on your chair as a signal to your server that you will be returning. Once the meal is over, place your napkin neatly on the table to the left of your dinner plate.

- Ordering – Look over the menu. If there are items you are uncertain about, ask your server any questions you may have. It is better to find out before you order that a dish is prepared with something you do not like or are allergic to than to spend the entire meal picking at your food. Order user-friendly foods that are easy to manage with a knife and fork. As a guest, you should not order the most expensive items on the menu or more than two courses, unless your hostess suggests you do otherwise. (Example: If the hostess says, "I'm going to try this delicious eight layer chocolate cake; why don't you try dessert, too?" or "The prime rib is the best in town. I think you would like it," then it is all right to order the item, if you would like.)

- "Mapping" the Table Setting – When traveling, we get roadmaps to insure where we are going and how to get there. We study the roadmaps before setting out for our destination. Are you frazzled with forks and goggle-eyed by glasses? Once you are seated, study the place setting carefully. It is possible to gain clues about what may be served by "mapping" the place setting. Start by drawing an imaginary line through the center of the serving plate. To the right of the imaginary line the following will be placed: glassware, cup and saucer, knives, and spoons (if the meal includes seafood, a seafood fork will be positioned on the soup spoon). To the left of the imaginary line the following will be placed: bread and butter plate (including small butter knife placed horizontally across the top of the plate), salad plate, napkin, and forks. In the event you really want to keep it simple, remember "B M W"– bread, meal, water. Bread to my left, meal in the middle, and water to my right. Should the person on your left unknowingly use your bread plate, don't acknowledge the faux pas. Resist the urge to tell them they messed up or to take the bread plate on your right and confuse others. Use your dinner plate for bread instead. And so it is with the water glass. If someone unknowingly uses your water glass, don't make a big deal out of it. Determine which has not been used or ask the server for a glass of water. (That's dignity.)

- Navigating the Silverware – Starting with the knife, fork, or spoon that is farthest from your plate, work your way in, using one utensil for each course. The salad fork is on your outermost left, followed by your dinner fork. Your soup spoon is on your outermost right, and then the salad knife and dinner knife. Your desert spoon and fork are above your plate or brought out with dessert. Remember, work from the outside in and you will be fine.

Informal Table Setting – bread, meal, water (BMW) placement

Informal Table Setting, Bread, meal, water (BMW) placement

Formal Table Setting

Formal Table Setting

- Holding Your Silverware – Holding the silverware correctly determines whether you go to the "Hall of Fame" or the "Hall of Shame". It is the most important thing to know when dining. Do not hold the fork like a shovel and the knife like a dagger. Let's practice: Open your hands, palms up. Place the knife and fork in your open hands. Let half of the handle of the knife and fork rest on the palm of each hand; the remainder should rest on your index fingers. Grasp the fork and knife and turn your hands over, resting your index fingers along the handles.

- Eating Styles – There are two ways to use a knife and fork and eat your food. Either style is considered appropriate.

  (1) American Style – One cuts the food by holding the knife in the right hand and the fork in the left hand with the fork tines piercing the food to secure it on the plate. Cut a bite-sized piece of food, and then lay your knife across the top edge of your plate with the sharp edge of the blade facing in. <u>Change your fork from your left to your right hand to eat, fork tines facing up</u>. (If you are left-handed, keep your fork in your left hand, tines facing up.)

  (2) Continental or European Style – The process is the same as the American style in that you cut your meat by holding your knife in your right hand, while securing your food with your fork in your left hand. <u>The difference is that your fork remains in your left hand, tines facing down, and the knife in your right hand</u>. Eat the cut pieces of food by picking them up with your fork still in your left hand.

As children grow up, the adults cut up all of the food at the beginning of the meal. Paradigm shift – with either style of eating, do not cut all of your food at once. Cut a bite-sized piece, lay your knife down, and eat the portion you have cut. Continue this process until you complete the meal. Remember, chew with your mouth closed; no gestures with the knife and fork. When pausing between bites or if you need to leave the table before completing the meal, place the knife and fork in the "rest" position. The "rest" position is the crossing of the fork and knife on your plate with the fork tines down, over the knife. Imagine an inverted "V". A trained server will not remove your plate with the fork and knife crossed. This is one of the silent codes of dining, indicating that the guest has not finished and is only resting. In the event the server does not understand the silent service code and attempts to remove your plate while you are still eating, quietly say, "I have not finished." (That's dignity.)

- **Bread and Butter** – The bread and butter plate is to your left. A bite-sized piece should be broken off and buttered on the butter plate. Each piece should be buttered as it is broken off to eat.

- **The Soup Course** – The soupspoon is held the same way a fork is held (steadied between your index finger and middle finger, and secured by your thumb). Contrary to what we frequently see, the soup is spooned away from you toward the center of the soup plate. It is sipped from the side of the spoon. (No slurping allowed.) The soup plate may be tipped away from you to get the last of the soup. If the soup is too hot, do not blow it to cool it down. Wait a few minutes before sipping.

- **When You Have Finished** – Leave your plate where it is in the place setting; do not push it away. Place the knife and fork in the "finished" position. (Another silent service code). The "finished" position is placing your knife and fork in the 10:20 position. Visualize the face of a clock on your plate. Place the fork and knife side by side in the approximate position of 10:20, with the tips of the fork and knife at 10 and the handles at 20. The tines of the fork may be placed up or down and the blade of the knife should face the fork. Make sure they are placed such that they do not slide off the plate as it is being removed.

Networking Etiquette

Networking is connecting. It is a natural extension of our innate talent to connect, collaborate, and communicate. Networking can be fun, or it might be intimidating. Learning and practicing effective networking techniques breaks down barriers and builds your confidence. It is knowing how to make conversation, where to go, keeping in touch, giving leads, and following up on leads. The two keys to successfully networking are **planning** and **preparation.**

Once it is determined you will attend an event, mark your calendar and prepare to go. Establish goals for attending the event. Be prepared with you business cards, a ready smile, interesting conversation topics, a concise self-introduction, and a goal. It is easier to network when you have a purpose, such as to meet seven new people, advertise my business, or find someone to build a website. Purpose helps you stay focused, and provides you with a goal to reach. Plan your wardrobe in advance so that you have appropriate clothing for the occasion, with easily accessible pockets, an interesting accessory to make you memorable (brooch, scarf), polished shoes, manicured hands, well-groomed hair, and a smile. A name tag is put on the right shoulder, where it can be easily seen.

When you meet someone and shake hands, their gaze will automatically follow your right arm up to your shoulder, then to your face. Keep your hands as free as possible. Hold food in your left hand to keep your right hand free for handshaking. When in a setting where there are appetizers to eat and beverages to drink as you circulate, enjoy the food and drink, but remember it is difficult to balance both a glass and a plate. Do not overload your plate. Be careful not to eat, drink, and talk at the same time. Avoid complaining about almost any subject, but especially about the room, food or attendees. Complaining leaves a negative impression with those you meet. Networking is an opportunity to meet people and sell your business and services. Be careful not to make it a sales pitch by pushing your business; it may alienate more people than you impress. Give yourself permission to talk to strangers and mingle with people you don't already know. Approach people who are standing alone. You will make them feel more comfortable, and your comfort level will rise as well. Exit a conversation graciously by simply saying, "It was a pleasure meeting you; enjoy the evening; shall we exchange cards?"

The key to successfully networking is "Follow-Up". Follow-up is the key to turning today's contacts into tomorrow's opportunities. Thank people immediately for referrals, resources, and support. Promptly send a note to everyone who is instrumental in helping you. Offer feedback to those who give you referrals or leads. When you meet new people, don't be self-serving by focusing only on your own business and needs. Share the time; find out what they need, and help them get what they want. Always remember that networking is a two-way process.

Seven Ways to Demonstrate Dignity and Grace

(1) **Be on time**. Punctuality shows that you are conscientious. Tardiness is very inconsiderate and implies that the other person's time is not valuable or they are not important.

(2) **Dress for the job you want, not the job you have**. Dress appropriately for your profession to increase your credibility. One's perception of your expertise comes in part from your appearance. Throw away the chewing gum; gum chewing can be very distracting and distasteful.

(3) **Have an attitude of gratitude**. Be courteous—Say "Please" and "Thank you", "You're Welcome" and "Excuse Me". Give compliments. Send handwritten thank you notes. These acts of kindness put you ahead of your competition, since most people don't make the extra effort.

(4) **Turn the cellular phone off** at public places such as the dinner, movies, church, concert, or the theatre. When your cellular phone is on, you feel a need to answer and act on calls, as if they are more urgent than your current activity. If you must accept a call, inform your host or guests when you sit down. When the phone rings, excuse yourself from the table, and keep the conversation private and brief.

(5) **Polish your speaking skills**. Develop a speaking style by selecting precise words, using complete sentences, speaking without slang and dialect, and using the appropriate language for the location. Act and speak in a formal way. Avoid profanity or language that is overly friendly or suggestive. It may be perceived as inappropriately familiar.

(6) **After hours, don't be too quick to let your hair down with co-workers.** In a relaxed atmosphere, tongues are loosened and guards are down. Don't believe that a conversation held off the premises is off the record. If you pass on a rumor, take potshots at an absent coworker or boss, or reveal a workplace confidence, what you said often gets back to the office before you.

(7) **Under promise and over produce.** Always deliver what you have promised and exceed the expectations of the recipient. (That's dignity and grace.)

The saying, "Manners open doors that position and money cannot" is true. Dignity and grace are powerful tools used to enhance your individuality. Power comes from knowledge. Knowledge builds confidence, and confidence builds leaders. Knowing what is proper conduct allows you to be comfortable and in control in any personal or business situation. There will be times when you step on toes, use the wrong fork, or forget an important name. It happens to the best of us. The important thing to remember is to strive to make people feel comfortable and valued. Your manners are always on display. Your future is often determined by how you conduct yourself in your relationships with other people. The Golden Rule: "Do unto others as your would have them do unto you", is the whole premise behind etiquette for today's woman. Accept the challenge to always walk in dignity and grace by continually improving your personal and business etiquette skills. By walking in dignity and grace, you enhance your natural beauty, and become elegant and eloquent women of purpose who are professional, productive, and polished.

Recommended reading

The Personal Touch by Terri Williams with Joe Cooney

Power Etiquette: What You Don't Know Can Kill Your Career by Dana May Casperson

The Little Book of Etiquette by Dorothea Johnson

Photo Credits:

Shon Smith – D' Angelo's Photos – Lakewood, California

This chapter is dedicated in loving memory to my mother, Louise Wade McNeese, who was an advocate of "good, better, best; never let it rest, for the good is the better and the better is the best."

Notes:

_____

_____

_____

_____

_____

_____

_____

_____

_____

_____

_____

_____

_____

_____

_____

_____

_____

_____

_____

_____

_____

ABOUT THE AUTHOR

KRISTI JOHNSON

As a successful writer, motivational speaker, life coach, consultant and seminar leader, Kristi Johnson has positively impacted the lives of thousands to achieve their personal and professional goals. Through the use of lessons learned through her own insightful experiences, she challenges others to find their voice and live their life the way God intended.

Johnson holds a B.A. in Mass Communications from Grambling State University and a M.A. in Speech Communications from Texas Southern University. She is member of The Professional Woman Network (PWN), National Association of Female Executives (NAFE), and Delta Sigma Theta Sigma Sorority, Inc.

Johnson is very active in her community, serving as a mentor for teenage girls at an area high school. She and husband, Jason reside in Houston, Texas and are members of Higher Dimension Church.

She is President and Founder of Johnson & Associates Consulting, a personal and professional development firm located in Houston, Texas. She is available for both national and international seminars and speaking engagements. Ms. Johnson served as co-author of Customer Service and Professionalism for Women, published by The Professional Woman Network.

Contact:
Kristi Johnson
Successfully Speaking
9396 Richmond Ave. #273
Houston, TX 77036
(281) 431-7606
info@successfullyspeaking.biz
www.successfullyspeaking.biz
www.protrain.net

TWO

IN SEARCH OF A GOOD MAN: FINDING A MATE FOR LIFE

By Kristi Johnson

Gather any group of African-American girlfriends together for a round table discussion on important issues and eventually the topic of relationships between men and women will certainly abound. For single black women who desire to one day unite in holy matrimony with a black male, it can sometimes seem to be a pipe dream in today's society, when considering the media's portrayal of our men. Staggering statistics constantly portray the African-American male as the "endangered black male", identifying him more often than not as undereducated, unemployed, prisoner or ex-prisoner, drug dealer or drug user, homosexual, living on the down low or dead. If you allow the media to shape your perception of today's black male, I must admit it can be discouraging to even the most optimistic soul.

While some single black women have surrendered their dreams of ever meeting "Mr. Right" in exchange for being content with "Mr. Right Now", other women have vowed to remain single and hopeful until their lifelong mate is identified. It matters not which category you are in. What does matter is that as a single black woman you continue to believe that a healthy, loving relationship with a black man can exist for you.

Despite the grim statistics, as a happily married African-American woman (to an African-American male) I do believe that it is possible to find a wonderful loving black man worthy of your love! Despite the negative messages communicated about the impossibility of black love and black relationships surviving and thriving, I still believe that black love is possible. Despite the many trials and tribulations that we have had to endure as a people that have damaged us psychologically and emotionally, black love is still very much alive. Despite stereotypes and myths about both black men and women, we are still finding the strength and courage to attempt to love one another. Although I have sister-friends that are either single, single with children, or married, I can honestly say that the majority of these friends are involved in loving relationships or marriages with good black men. When I think of all the loving black marriages that exist, despite what statistics report, it gives me hope for all the single sisters who are still waiting to be embraced by a love second only to the love of God; a love that is true, unconditional, unwaivering, and unbreakable.

Now by no means do I intend to paint a fairy tale picture of a blissful marriage completely devoid of any challenging issues or problems, because every marriage has them. As African-American men and women, we are constantly battling with the pain caused by our history, struggling to navigate the path to reconnecting in order to form trusting, loving bonds again.

My intentions are simply to remind and encourage any single sister that desires a loving relationship with a black man that it is possible, simply because God tells us in his Holy Word that, if you seek Him first, He will give you the desires of your heart.

The beautiful biblical love story of Ruth and Boaz found in the book of Ruth confirms that God does recognize our desires for a husband. Ruth was a poor, selfless widow who left her country to go and care for her mother-in-law. There, while focusing on serving God, He blessed her with a wonderful, loving husband named Boaz, a Godly and wealthy landowner. (I encourage you to read this story in its entirety if you have not done so, as it can serve as an excellent source of inspiration as to what God is capable of doing regarding relationships.) No matter what society says we should do in terms of finding true love, you can stand firm on God's word and have faith that at the appointed time He will allow you to meet your Boaz.

Now I know that some of you are thinking deep down inside that God must not hear your prayers, so I'll just help Him out a little by attempting to expedite this match-making process. Well, take it from me, a married woman who for years was convinced that God must have been ignoring my desires for marriage. So, I took it upon myself to organize and command "Operation Find–A–Husband!" Each strategy I implemented seemed to fail, and I became frustrated with God, depressed with my life, and angry with my boyfriend (who is my husband now).

It wasn't until one evening when I was leaving my boyfriend's apartment that a change truly occurred. Although he had never verbally expressed his recognition of my insecurities and lack of self-love, he knew as well as I did through my actions that I was completely lost. As I left, he handed me something that changed the course of my life and our relationship. It was a small piece of paper with a list of scriptures about love. I was blown away. After I arrived home, I dusted off my Bible (that's right, I had not read it in quite awhile) and began to read the scriptures he listed. As I read about God's love for me, tears began to flow down my face because I realized that I had become so engulfed with the idea of being married, that I had begun to totally neglect myself, my growth in God, and my Bible. Even though I was reared in church and raised to believe in God, I had gone completely astray, as many of us do in search of a self-fulfilling prophecy.

The dust on my Bible was symbolic of the dust that had accumulated within my comatose soul. On the exterior my life looked great, I was an educated, employed, single black female with family and friends who loved me. However, I lacked love for myself. Inside I was completely empty; I had become consumed with my obsession of finding love and marriage.

That night served as a major turning point. I realized that, no matter what you do–giving more in relationships than you should, putting all his needs before your own, neglecting family and friends to spend time with your man, looking good, smelling good, candle-lit bubble baths, sex before marriage, those jeans that fit just right–none of these things will lead to a successful relationship or a fulfilling, lifelong marriage. It will only leave you feeling empty and shallow inside!

Being a beautiful woman and having a voluptuous body will not guarantee happiness in a marriage! It is only after you begin to understand who you are in God that you can find true love. So instead of "searching" for a man, allow the real "search" to begin with you. Be patient and pray for discipline to redirect your focus toward God. Vow to begin a journey of self–discovery (or rediscovery), a journey well worth the travel. It is a journey that will eventually lead you to the love that you are so worthy of. You can have the love you so deeply desire, but it all starts with you!

Allow the focus of your "search" to begin with God, and then "search" the other areas listed below. It will eventually lead you to your lifelong mate.

1). **"Search" for the love of God.** Before you can find the love you desire from a man, you must first seek God and understand how much God loves you. In fact, his love is much deeper than any human relationship you will ever experience! The Bible tells us in Matthew 6:33 (NIV) that we should "Seek ye first his kingdom and his righteousness, and all these things will be given to you." As his children, Psalms 139:14 assures us, "We are all fearfully and wonderfully made in your God's image." You must understand that no matter what mistakes you have made in the past, no matter how many times you've allowed yourself to go against his will both knowingly and unknowingly, HE STILL LOVES YOU BEYOND MEASURE!! As unbelievable as it may seem, he loves you and nothing in your past or present can change that, even that thing you used to do, that you can't believe you ever did, and vowed to never do again. Yes, that! He knows about it, still loves you, and still wants to make you whole again! You are still worthy of love! Forgive yourself, repent, learn from the past, and let it go!! I can't tell you how much time I wasted beating myself up inside for mistakes

I made. I finally realized that I was worthy of God's love, just as you are, simply because you were created by God. Remember, God created each one of us, and nobody, I repeat nobody, is without sin! The scriptures below demonstrate God's awesome love for you:

1) *Psalms 100:5 – For the Lord is good and his love endures forever; his faithfulness continues through all generations.*

2) *Psalms 86:13 – For great is your love toward me; you have delivered me from the depths of the grave.*

3) *Psalms 107:8-9 – Let them give thanks to the Lord for His unfailing love and His wonderful deeds for men, for it satisfies the thirsty and fills the hungry with good things.*

Exercise

List below anything that you need to forgive yourself for:

1. _____

2. _____

3. _____

2). "Search" for the real you. Be honest with yourself. Do you really know who you are? Do you define yourself with other's perceptions of you? Do you allow others to box you into their definition of what they think you should be? It is absolutely impossible to understand what you desire or need from a mate if you don't fully know yourself. Take some time to identify your attributes and qualities. When we don't truly know and accept ourselves, there is room for insecurities to creep into our thoughts, when others attempt to impose their opinions upon us, causing us to waiver in our own beliefs. When you don't define who you are, you leave the door wide open for any man that comes into your life to define you. As black women, we are a beautiful, resilient, vibrant, innovative group of women who deserve the best in every aspect of our lives. You must understand your worth and value before you can recognize a black man who is worthy of your love. Recognizing what you value most in a mate begins with identifying those things that are most important to you. Answer the following questions as honestly as possible:

1) Do I truly understand my worth as a child of God?

2) What do I value in my friendships?

3) What do I value most in life?

4) What are my religious beliefs?

5) What strengths do I like most about me?

6) What weaknesses do I honestly need to improve?

7) What issues am I sensitive about?

8) What issues do I need to address from my past, in order to prevent it from affecting my future relationship?

9) In what ways am I working to reinvent myself?

10) What are my short-term and long-term goals?

11) What are my greatest fears and why? How can I learn to overcome those fears?

3). "Search" for opportunities to grow. Seek ways to constantly improve yourself as a person. Don't be afraid to try new activities that you normally wouldn't do. This allows you to broaden your horizons and possibly discover new interests. When you do, you will so proud of yourself! Even if it's a little scary, or something that causes you to move from your comfort zone, jump at the chance to learn more about who you are. I strongly believe that when you already have an active life before you meet your mate, you will be more likely to continue those activities rather than waiting around to for him to plan your daily schedule. Remember, a successful marriage involves two people who both bring their interests to the table. Even when you become a married woman, although you and your husband will develop activities you enjoy together, you should never, ever lose yourself and forget your own interests. Below are a few suggestions of things that might interest you. And remember, give it a try before you decide against it. Who knows, you might just meet a potential mate while learning something new!

1) Visit museums or art galleries.

2) Take a photography class.

3) Learn to speak another language.

4) Volunteer with a charitable organization.

5) Train for a marathon.

6) Go bike riding.

7) Learn to bowl.

8) Volunteer with a political campaign.

9) Take a dance class (ballroom, salsa hip-hop, jazz, tap).

10) Learn to scuba dive (for the really daring sisters!)

4). "Search" for wisdom. Simply stated, be careful who you accept
   advice from. When you understand who you are, what you are
   worth, and what you deserve, you will better equipped to identify
   good advice and advice that you just allow to travel in one ear and
   out the other. Most of us within the African-American culture have
   been raised to respect the opinions of our elders and seek their
   advice on challenging issues that we will encounter during our
   life's journey. I will be the first to agree with the fact that many
   of our mothers, grandmothers and great grandmothers all possess
   great wisdom that you won't find in a textbook. However, it's also
   important to keep in mind that older age does not always equal
   wisdom. I've learned that just because a person is an elder doesn't
   mean that they are wise in all areas of their lives.

It is so important to surround yourself with other people who
possess a positive attitude toward marriage and relationships. Try your
best to avoid anyone who has a negative opinion about the success
of relationships. When accepting advice from others, always examine
their relationship first. Be certain that they are involved in or have been
involved in the type of relationship you are seeking. Ask yourself the
following questions:

1) Does this person truly have my best interest at heart?

2) Does this person value and love themselves?

3) Would this person ever intentionally jeopardize my relationship?

4) Is this person or has this person ever been involved in a happy monogamous relationship?

5) Does this person's marriage exemplify the qualities I desire in a healthy relationship?

5). "Search" for the strength to set boundaries. In order for anyone to respect you, you must first respect yourself. The ability to establish boundaries within your relationship communicates to your mate that you love and respect yourself greatly, and are unwilling to compromise those things that are important to you. Many men will determine how they treat you by trying to test your boundaries and observing the way you respond. It could be something as simple as calling your home after a certain time each night, or standing you up for a date and then sporadically dropping by whenever he pleases. In these situations, do you: a) go along with whatever he chooses to do? Or b) firmly explain to him that if he can't respect your rules, then you should probably not continue the relationship.

Establishing boundaries from the very beginning will lay the foundation for the entire relationship. Men want to know that you have a backbone. Men do not want a woman that will allow them to run over you!

There is another very important area that definitely requires boundaries. That's right, sisters you must set boundaries with your body. Let's be quite honest. For many of us, this is or was one of the hardest areas to enforce our boundaries, myself included. We live in a sex-driven society. Our world is inundated with sexual messages and images all day, everyday. Learning the value of who you are and what you deserve can greatly increase your ability to resist the temptation of temporary sexual gratification. Ask God for the strength to stand firm in your belief that God will reward you for your obedience with a wonderful, loving mate created for you.

Remember, this is your commitment with God, not a commitment with a man. You must trust God to place someone in your life who will respect your choices and commitment. Based upon my own personal mistakes, it would definitely be worth the wait. And yes, sister you are worth the wait!

6). **"Search" the man's heart and mind.** Take your time getting to know a potential mate. Learn to look past the superficial things that will eventually fade away. For example, I'm sure many sisters will agree that we *love* a well-dressed brother. A brother in a suit, looking good and smelling good, will obviously attract many women. But once you get past the initial attraction, you should then be prepared with a list of questions that either qualify or disqualify him as a potential mate. Here's a list of "qualifying questions" you should always consider:

1) Does he believe in God?

2) How does he treat his mother?

3) What are his views of women in general?

4) Is he family oriented?

5) Does he have goals for the future? Is he doing anything to further those goals?

6) Does he communicate his thoughts and feelings in an effective manner?

7) Does he possess a good work ethic?

8) Have you ever observed him demonstrating any physically, emotionally or verbally abusive behavior?

9) Does he respect himself?

10) Are you high on his priority list?

11) Is he healthy? Do you know his HIV status? Does he have any other physical or mental conditions that could affect your relationship?

12) Does he handle his financial responsibilities?

Also consider any other areas that are of importance to you. The more you come to know yourself, your worth, and what you are truly deserving of, the more you will be able to better identify the best mate for you. Commit to never settle for less than the best in your life. This journey may be longer for some sisters than others. To be honest, it seemed like an eternity for me. But there is no better feeling that walking down the aisle on your wedding day with no regrets, knowing that you have found your true love, your Boaz…and it all began by not searching for the man, but by searching within yourself.

ABOUT THE AUTHOR

DAWN HARRIS

Ms. Harris is President and CEO of The Harris Institute for Professional Excellence. She received her MBA from Woodbury University in Burbank, California and her undergraduate degree in Biochemistry at the Cal Poly State University in San Luis Obispo, California. Ms. Harris has worked in the Medical Device industry as a Manager of Regulatory Training. Prior to this capacity, she worked in the biotechnology industry for over nine years in a variety of departments such as Quality Assurance, Manufacturing, Internal Audit, and Corporate Finance.

As a Certified Customer Service Trainer, Dawn Harris is committed to teaching individuals the importance of a professional image, positive attitude development, and business etiquette. As a Certified Diversity Trainer, she is passionate about training companies and individuals regarding the importance of exclusivity vs. inclusivity, and building teams among diverse corporate cultures. Ms. Harris has co-authored *Customer Service & Professionalism for Women* and *The Young Woman's Guide for Personal Success.*

Contact:
The Harris Institute for Professional Excellence
(443) 266-4066
dharris@theharrisinstitute.com
www.protrain.net

THREE

OVERCOMING LIFE'S TRAGEDIES

By Dawn M. Harris

Tragedies, struggles and strife do not respect the sanctity of the individual. They happen to the rich, the middle class, the working poor, the young, the old, the "good" and the "bad" people of this world. How do we know this? We know this because there is not one documented case of a person buying their way out of a tragic experience, too old to experience tragedy, or being so nice that tragedy never comes their way.

The following statistics prove that hard times can affect women no matter their race, income, or age. Consider these facts provided by the International Society for Mental Health (ISMH) and the Nutrition Health Care Center:

- In the United States, women are twice as likely as men to be diagnosed and treated for major depression.

- Approximately 20-25% of women and 12% of men will experience a serious episode of depression at least once in their lifetime.

- Approximately 7 million women in the United States are clinically depressed.

- One in five women can expect to develop clinical depression at some time in her life.

- Almost 15 percent of women suffering from severe depression will commit suicide.

- Nearly 10 percent of women will experience postpartum depression in the months following the birth of a child.

- Married women have higher rates of depression than single women, with depression most likely during childbearing years.

- Depression in women occurs most frequently between the ages of 25 and 44.

These statistics are staggering! The most unfortunate aspect about depression, in my opinion, is that it is not fully known what exactly causes clinical depression. It could be a number of things ranging from biological and genetic factors, environmental influences, or attributable to a childhood or developmental event(s). However, it is most likely caused by the influence of multiple factors.

Studies have shown that a person whose mother had reoccurring bouts of depressive episodes may have inherited a vulnerability to developing clinical depression (genetic influence). If someone with such a family history, combined with low self-esteem (psychological influence), happened to be going through a divorce (environmental influence), their response to stress may predispose them to experiencing depression compared to someone else with a different set of influences.

It has been my experience that what people think about themselves (their self-perception) is the root of depression and anxiety. Negative thoughts form the confines within which their ability to overcome tragedy or misfortune is severely impacted.

Coupled with our thoughts, depression is our body's response to tragedy. It is a proven fact, as articulated by ISMH, that our immune system is compromised when we are under stress. As our physical and psychological responses are closely related (mind and body), it follows that once we choose our attitude, our body follows its lead. For example, one can control their blood pressure if they choose to work out and eat better. Likewise, the attitude with which we choose to manage conflict or adversity determines whether depression sets in or the "fight" in us comes out. It's not what happens to a person, it is how they choose to deal with what is happening or has happened to them.

To activate the process of overcoming, we cannot begin with the end in mind. I believe that we have to start where we are mentally. Our prior experiences prepare us for the next misfortune (whether that is a divorce or a death, we leverage off of our past knowledge of life-changing events to move forward emotionally). This is what I define as our internal coping mechanism.

Each of us has a different threshold when it comes to the amount of disappointment, stress, trauma or grief we can endure. So, what may seem like a "light storm" for one person may be viewed as a "hurricane" to another. One possible example would be losing a job. One person may see this as cataclysmic, thereby, placing their lives in desperate peril. Another person however, may view the same event as a chance to take some well-deserved time off for travel or spend time with the kids. It all depends on their attitude and outlook towards a given situation.

Nevertheless, it takes time to recover and heal from life-altering experiences. Therefore, it is important to be upfront and honest with yourself when you are staring into the stark face of tragedy. In order to overcome it, you have to know how it rates on <u>your</u> scale of impact then work towards a strategy to overcome it. It is easy to be overwhelmed with useless advice from well-meaning family members and friends that consider your "hurricane" to be a "light storm". They will say things like, "It's not that bad." "Don't worry about it; things like this happen all the time." Oh yeah? Well thanks for downgrading my Category 5 hurricane! I feel much better now! (You actually walk away feeling more embarrassed than emboldened.)

It's a completely different story when someone tries to help you "reframe" your situation so that you can more accurately rank its significance and move forward. They will ask questions instead of providing instant solutions. For example, they may ask the following:

- How does this event affect your ability to continue to reach your goals?

- What can I do to help?

- What is the core issue for you within this situation?

- Do you see a way out?

- Do you think you are going to need professional advice or help?

I feel that it is imperative to seek outside support to help someone see the opportunities that await after every tragedy. After my most recent "opportunity", I will never look at tragedy the same again.

In September of 2005, I was blown out of the water by a company lay-off. The company determined that it had to cut back due to the over-production of equipment and lack of sales. While the executive staff received bonuses, I along with approximately thirty other employees received boxes. This was considered a Category 5 hurricane for me. I was numb when I got the news from my manager. In a matter of minutes, my life took a turn and it has never been the same since.

Needless to say, I called everyone who would listen and told them about how devastated I was and asked how could this happen at such a vulnerable time. At the time I was staying with a friend temporarily as I was in the process of buying a home. One week prior to my lay-off, I had made the last payment on my deposit for a new town home.

All I could think of was how much I loved my job and that I just didn't know what I was going to do! From my vantage point, it was a series of calamities; I lost my home, my job, my ability to become an instructor at a neighboring university, my salary, my peace of mind, my value and my stability.

As I spoke to each friend and family member, I witnessed something that only few people get to see in a lifetime. It was the outpouring of advice, kindness, love, attention and generosity that only people with favor from above will experience. And boy was it abundant!

I cried. I laughed. I was angry and frustrated, but it was all to be temporary. The beauty of the whole situation was that I had an opportunity to start over. I was able to reestablish myself in a better place, closer to family, and focus on building my business. Although that was not my initial reaction, the opportunities revealed themselves as time moved on.

Exercise

List some of the tragedies that you have experienced in your lifetime:

_____

_____

_____

_____

What was your reaction to them?

_____

_____

_____

_____

How did you overcome them?

_____

_____

_____

_____

I believe we learn from tragedy by replaying the mental tape that has recorded the traumatic memory in our mind. We rewind and play the tape, not to continue to hurt ourselves, or make us feel down, but to truly embrace the opportunity on the other side of that point in time.

Eventually the tape that is played in our mind will become a touchstone of strength for us. We can look back on that situation and say to ourselves, "Look how strong I was!" or "Look how gracefully I handled that!" Then we can share the tragedies of our lives with others, not to get sympathy but to encourage and strengthen others. It can help others to gain a new perspective and see how difficult situations can be dealt with and eventually worked out.

There are healthy and unhealthy ways of dealing with misfortunes, but it takes a willing spirit and creativity to break out of one's normal approach to tragedy and apply a more positive and healthy approach to it. The greatest living example of this is my sister. In my opinion, she is one of the strongest women I know, because of what she has endured over the last two years.

In June of 2004, my sister received a phone call that every mother dreads; it was from my aunt regarding my sister's son. He was being detained in the county jail because of an incident that had occurred two weeks prior to his arrest. In a firm tone and a strong voice, my sister alerted the family via a conference call on my nephew's situation.

Shortly thereafter, my sister and I flew out to collect my nephew's clothing from the apartment he was living in. As we collected his belongings, I could not help feeling as though he were dead. I kept glancing at my sister as I placed his clothing, shoes and cologne in trash bags to store at my aunt's house. I was waiting for her to find something that was going to send her over the edge and make her dash out of the dilapidated apartment in tears, but she didn't. Relieved, and fighting the lump in my throat, I kept filling the trash bags. My nephew was released on bail and was placed under house arrest at my aunt's home until his arraignment.

In November of 2004, two day's before Thanksgiving, my nephew was sentenced to five years in prison. Although there were tears shed by all, I never thought I would witness my sister receive a hopeless situation with such grace and peace. She did not yell, scream or curse anyone. She stood and bared it.

At the time, I could only imagine what could have been going through her mind when the Judge called on my nephew to plead his case. Simply stating that it was 'hard' or a 'rough time' would not fully describe the anxiety and tension of this moment. It had to be heart wrenching and more damaging than a raging fire to have to sit and watch your child become property of the state. It is like watching a child from a distance take a hard fall and not being able to do one thing about it.

How did she resist the overwhelming temptation to hold her son as he recounted the events of the evening that lead to him robbing three college students (at gun point) to gain a total of $40.00? How did she gain the energy and strength to hug her son goodbye after his sentence, while he was handcuffed and could not hug her in return? How did she return to work, not knowing when she would speak to or hear from her son again? How does she continue to enjoy life, mindful of her son, but pressing as though he were free? No parent is prepared for this type of situation.

My sister had a choice to make. She either had to get busy living, or get busy dying, (as Morgan Freeman said in *Shawshank Redemption*). A lot of mothers do the time with their child. In other words, they stay in the doldrums until their child is released, whether it is two months or twenty years. I am proud to say, my sister is not doing that. She chose God. She chose to seek a higher power to ease the pain and the despair in her life. She chose to be an "over-comer" and not a victim of someone else's circumstance. She chose life instead of death.

While others were sharing their faithless stories with her about what happened to their child or friend that went into a maximum-security prison and never came out, or how the judge is not going to be lenient because a gun was involved, my sister remained faithful. Regardless of what the situation looked like on the outside, she was expecting God to show up and show favor on her son's behalf.

My nephew is still incarcerated, but he will not have a record upon his release and is not serving his sentence it in a maximum-security prison. He is in a correctional training center where he is well supervised and protected from harm.

For some, my sister's testimony may be simply another day in the life of someone's son or relative "that caught a case". For my sister and my family, it was sobering. This is not a common occurrence in my family by any stretch of the imagination. It was horrifying, saddening, awkward, uncomfortable and emotionally taxing for all of us.

Exercise

Have you ever had to support someone through a tragedy? If so, what did you learn?

_____

_____

_____

_____

Based on your answer(s) above, were you able to apply what you learned to your own life? If not, what might you be holding onto that may not be allowing you to?

_____

_____

_____

_____

As I mentioned earlier, your mindset is key to being an "overcomer". Your view of yourself will determine your ability to withstand or be defeated by tragedy and by extension, depression. Knowing that tragedy is temporary and that we must learn from it is hard to apply when you are in "the storm". It is best to start thinking in this manner prior to experiencing your next misfortune.

As we move through the storm, it is important to find your support group, people you can lean on emotionally and physically (i.e. staying with someone temporarily if need be). Take this time to find a way to view adversity as an opening to the possibility to learn and grow on a personal, as well as spiritual level. It is at that point we can truly conquer that which may have intended to conquer us.

I do not believe any of us really knows what is inside us until we are tested. In my view, that is the hidden beauty of adversity or tragedy.

Whenever I go through or witness rough periods in life, I remember what my dad taught me after I was dismissed from college, for the *second* time (but who's counting). He asked me if I knew how precious diamonds were made. At the time, I thought it was the most ridiculous question (sorry Daddy)! I could not for the life of me understand at that moment, what diamonds had to do with dismissals–but I was curious!

With my curiosity peaked and my head hung low, I fought back the tears over the phone and said in a low voice, "No." I could hear him smiling over the phone, knowing in the back of his mind that his explanation would get me back "on top" of things! With the proper response received, he sighed and said, "Diamonds are formed when a lot of pressure and heat are applied. If that environment is not created over time, a diamond cannot be made. It is just like the process of forming a precious metal, honey. It is only formed when heat is applied; it is shaped and then polished. If it does not happen in that order, it is not considered precious."

He asked me to remember that and to look at all of my obstacles in life as refining moments, not defining moments, because they are opportunities to be shaped and polished. So I did and still do.

As I close out this chapter, I would like to leave you with a list of personal "pearls of wisdom" I wear and share:

- Tragedy and adversity are TEMPORARY. So don't take on a permanent negative attitude in response to something that is temporary.

- Find a circle – Surround yourself with people that are supportive and do not down play your "storm".

- Get busy – Keep planning and strategizing on ways to make your current situation better. Plant the seeds today for tomorrow's harvest!

- Get focused – Concentrate on the things you can control. Write down your long-term goals.

- Keep believing in YOU. Remember that you are the most important factor during any time of adversity. Remind yourself that you are an over-comer and may have to endure this rough period now, but will be victorious in the end.

- Keep walking – When you are "going through hell", don't stop and ask for ice water. Stay focused on doing what will make your tomorrow brighter.

- Your misery can be your ministry – Once you get through your "valley", you can help others going through what you have been through.

- Overtime, being bitter decreases your friendship circle and prohibits goodness to come into your life.

- Your pain is preparation for your destiny – The character you are building now is going to come in handy later.

- Life is about loss just as much as it is about gain.

- Your 'set back' is the doorway to your 'set-up'!

- Find or write affirmations that you can read daily.

- Never give up – keep fighting. Press!!

Notes:

ABOUT THE AUTHOR

Sharon M. Hudson

Dr. Sharon M. Hudson is a corporate trainer and an Adjunct Professor. She facilitates education and training via face-to-face, blended courses and online. She provides coaching to employees and students to increase their knowledge, competencies, and skills to ensure their marketability in this fast-changing environment.

She has participated in an international exchange of information with a focus on the adult learner with universities and social service organizations in South Africa. She has her own business, Hudson Institute for Excellence, with a focus on Coaching, Diversity and Women's Issues, and Leadership.

Dr. Hudson's formal education includes a Baccalaureate degree in Liberal Arts, a Master of Arts degree in Communication, Governors State University, and a Doctorate in Adult Continuing Education, Northern Illinois University.

She is a member of Professional Woman Network, National Association of Female Executives, American Association of University Women, and the American Society for Training and Development.

Contact
Dr. Sharon M. Hudson
Hudson Institute for Excellence
15774 S. LaGrange Road #250
Orland Park, IL 60462
(708) 227-3737
sharon_hudson@sbcglobal.net
www.protrain.net

FOUR

TAKING CONTROL: PERSONAL LEADERSHIP SKILLS

By Dr. Sharon M. Hudson

It was a warm summer day. The sun was shining, birds singing, and there was a slight breeze in the air. I exited the building, was walking towards my car and gazing at the structural and leafy surroundings. Then it hit me. It was like a mild slap in the face. I am in the cockpit of a Boeing 737. What is my flight plan? There are many gauges and instruments facing me. I don't know the function of most of these instruments, but I'm about to find out.

The day arrived when I would embark out on my own into that wide-open sky of life. Was it scary? Yes. Was it exciting? Yes. For me, it was another new adventure. Would I survive? I had to. The transition was not as scary for me as I thought it would be. In the beginning, I would sometimes wonder if I should be more frazzled than I was. That thought never lasted long and I knew why. Based on some of the events that have happened in my life, I knew God was with me. I knew I would be okay. I had no illusions that this new adventure would be smooth. I also knew I was going to encounter some turbulence that would scare me.

Okay, so here I am in this cockpit. What now? What do I do first? There are three choices. First, I can take control and decide the destiny of this plane, my life. Second, I can let someone else control my destiny. Finally, I could just sit in the cockpit and wait for something to happen, and then react to it.

I was scared, unsure of what path to take and the outcome, and wanted the comfort of experience to guide me. All of these factors make it easy to allow someone else to control my destiny; easy to sit back and do nothing. During my conversations with myself, I thought, if I don't do anything, this excludes me from making decisions, mistakes, taking action, or being accountable and responsible for my own life. If (and when) something goes wrong, it is not my fault. I also thought if I do this, life may not turn out the way I want it to and I can blame others and circumstances for the way my life turns out. Did I want this? No!

Let me give you a little insight about myself. While discovering life, I was also discovering who I am. I learned that I am not part of the in-crowd, and I am comfortable with that. I never tried to fit in. Sometimes I will purposely make sure I don't fit in. I enjoy a good challenge! I learned I have to have peace, joy, and happiness in my life, and what my values are.

Getting to know myself included:

- Listening to my inner voice

- Reflecting on my experiences and attaching meaning to them

- Defining my values, beliefs, goals, and vision for myself

- Being open-minded

- Taking risks (realizing I will make mistakes and should not be too critical of myself)

- Learning I had to be responsible and accountable for my actions without creating excuses

- Taking action and making revisions when necessary

- Obtaining results

- Welcoming change

- Enjoying life

I quickly discovered I was not (and am not) one for letting others decide what I will do or not do. Therefore, the second choice was not an option. Don't get me wrong though. Growing up I obeyed my parents. There was very little room (if any) to get out of line. When I got out of line (a few times), there was no doubt about the consequences.

My interactions with others and my years as a student helped me to discover my communication, personality, listening, and behavioral styles. My years as an Adjunct Professor allowed me to enlighten others about their various styles. Knowing this information enhances your relationships (especially the ones you're committed to) with others. Helping others gives me great satisfaction!

I don't like to wait. My patience is very thin. Therefore, the last choice was not an option. I was not going to sit around and wait for something to happen. I quickly learned the functions of those various gauges in that Boeing 737 that represented the various aspects of life. I'm not saying it was easy, nor am I saying everything turned out the way I wanted it to. Things turned out for the best. You know how you want something very much and don't get it? Reflecting back on some of the things I wanted and didn't get, I know it was for the best. If it was not in God's plan for me to have something, I didn't get it. Because I do get impatient sometimes, God made me have patience. I am very grateful and feel very blessed for that. Looking back, had God not stepped in, I would have been in a few situations that I did not want to be in. After experiencing some things in life, a few questions came up.

Taking Control

Where do I start? How do I take and keep control? How do I handle what life gives me? As mentioned previously, I knew God was with me. I'm not saying I stayed in church or was part of the choir. This is the foundation I built upon which helped me to stay on the right path. It was not easy, but it wasn't difficult to the extent I couldn't handle it. I made a choice. Choosing God as my foundation meant not swaying in every direction. It was not an option to be on both sides of the fence, nor in the middle. Choosing God also meant I would be tempted. It meant knowing right from wrong and choosing to do what's right. Choosing to do what's right is not a popular decision and sometimes very difficult. I'm okay with that because, depending on the situation, I don't always like to conform.

I wondered sometimes about certain decisions I made. If I solicited the advice of someone else (a few times I did), I'd critically evaluate what was said, the situation, and made the best decision I could. It was sometimes kind of scary and exciting at the same time. But I was comfortable in making decisions because I was comfortable with me. **Tip:** Be careful whom you solicit information from. Not everyone has your best interest at heart. People have their own agendas and will intentionally try to make you stumble. You have to discover and weed out these people, or at least know how to handle them.

During those turbulent moments, it was harder to stand. I asked myself, "Why should I be concerned about staying on the right path?" I saw how others were having it easier than I was, so it seemed. But I found out they were not. When I had thoughts of not doing what I knew to be the right thing, they did not last long. God always threw something in my path to bring me back to my senses. I am grateful and thankful for that. Where do you start? With God! You must build your foundation in the Word. *"Your word is a lamp to my feet and a light for my path."* (Psalm 119:105).

In addition to having God as your foundation, get to know you. What do you like or dislike? What are you willing to accept and not accept? What do you want to do with your life? Take time for you. Take time to laugh, even at yourself sometimes. Accept who you are (don't keep comparing yourself to others). God created you in his image and you are unique. Love yourself! God does! Getting to know yourself builds self-confidence and instills in you other characteristics that will help you succeed in life. What is success? You have to define what this is for you. You also have to know your values, beliefs, goals, and have a vision for yourself.

Values

What are your values? What do you rate as highly important to you? The responses to these questions must be yours, not someone else's. What you rate as highly important is where you spend your time and what your energy goes into. Your values will <u>manifest</u> in what you do with your life.

I won't list them all, but some of my values include:

- Peace of mind

- Integrity

- Honesty

- Keeping my word

- Ability to help others

- Commitment, perseverance

- Courage, conviction

Beliefs

Beliefs are your assumptions about life, people, etc. What do you believe to be true? Your cultural background and what you learned as a child contributes to your beliefs. As we mature, experience new things, interact with others, and travel to different places, your beliefs can be challenged. However, with an open mind, your beliefs can be enlightened.

Goals

As with values, the goals you have must be yours, not someone else's. Identify the purpose of your goals to know why you're trying to achieve them. Goals are easy to set, sometimes difficult to accomplish, and may have to be revised periodically. You may have long and short-term goals. For example, one long-term goal I had was to complete a doctoral program, a long process. So that it would not be too overwhelming, I broke it up into smaller steps. Complete an Associates Degree, Bachelor's Degree, and Master's degree (and then the Doctorate). I use a simple chart (below) to map out my future goals and make sure it's easily accessible for review and/or revision. Create your own chart or use this one, but do have a plan.

My Goals

Long Term Goals

Description	Resources	Complete by

Short Term Goals

Description	Resources	Complete by

A long-term goal can be broken down into several short-term goals. This helps you realize you are making progress. Please do not get discouraged if you need to revise your plan. Remain focused, and do not allow yourself to be easily distracted. It's okay to get derailed for a few days, but get back on track. Be realistic. Don't set out to be a pilot in three months. You'll only create unnecessary turbulence for yourself.

You will feel really great about yourself each time you complete a short-term goal that gets you closer to achieving your long-term goal. Celebrate your achievements. Depending on your immediate circle of family and friends, you may not think you should celebrate. You may feel a little guilty about celebrating, or you may feel guilty about the success in your life. You're human; it's okay to feel this because you want the best for others (especially those close to you). You want them to have successes to celebrate. If they don't, keep in mind we all have the opportunity to set and achieve goals. This is not an easy process, and some people are able to withstand the obstacles that arise in trying to achieve goals more so than others. Do not judge or devalue others because of what they may not have achieved. Everyone has value. It is up to those that can climb a treacherous mountain to help those that struggle or can't climb.

Vision

What mental image do you have for yourself in the future? What is your passion? What do you want to do with your life? Answer these questions and you will discover your vision! Your vision can come from a combination of sources such as paying attention to your goals, listening to your inner thoughts and the comments of others, and observing the world around you. Nurturing these sources will help form your vision. It is up to you, though, to bring it to <u>fruition.</u>

Personal Leadership Toolkit

Personal leadership requires you to have certain tools/attributes/ characteristics in your leadership toolbox. In addition to values, beliefs, goals, and a vision, the following are some characteristics you'll need in your leadership toolkit to lead yourself first and then others. These characteristics are visible to others. They are:

Attitude – *a mental position or feeling.* Are you an optimist or pessimist? Which attitude do you choose to own? Don't try to blame life if you have a pessimistic attitude. You will encounter heartache, pain, and disappointments. You will also experience happiness, laughter, feeling good about yourself, gratitude, and personal accomplishments. Your attitude is reflected in everything you do. It is totally your choice. Make it a positive one!

Character – *distinguishing feature, attribute.* Your character is part of who you are. Your actions make up your character. You build character, whether weak or strong, each day of your life. You've probably heard the phrase, "It's easier said than done." This is so true. Your character is who you are when no one's watching.

When you encounter a difficult situation, how do you handle it? Do you take the easy way out? Do you speak the truth, do what's right, and carry the weight of it? Do you manipulate the truth because it's easier to do so? How do you present yourself to the world? It is your choice how you build your character.

Courage – *ability to conquer fear or despair, bravery.* You have to be able to face your challenges. Let go of the familiar. This is more important than the fear of doing this.

Commitment – *to pledge or assign to some particular course or use.* What are you committed to? Is it productive? Whatever it is, stick to your plan. It may have to be revised periodically. Some very difficult situations can possibly come your way and knock you down. Will you stay down? How many times can you tolerate being knocked down? Do you have the heart to be knocked down and get back up?

Focus – *center attention on.* What plans do you have for your life? What do you want to accomplish? Is there something about yourself you would like to change for the better? Is there something you want to do to help others? Take time to identify what you want and concentrate on that. On occasion, you'll wonder if it's worth it or not. I have and probably will again. Believe me, it is worth it!

Listen – *pay attention to in order to hear.* Pay attention to your inner voice. Be aware of how you think of and treat yourself. We tend to be more critical of ourselves. If you're really critical of yourself, what can be done to change this? Something as simple as changing words you use (from negative to positive, from I can't to I can) can change how you view yourself and how you feel about yourself. Keep positive thoughts about yourself and what you can do. When you feel good about yourself it shows, and you treat others positively.

Desire for lifelong learning – *gaining knowledge, understanding, or skill.* Learning is such a joy and there's no age limit to it. I seek opportunities to learn something new. In this fast pace of economic and technological advancements, you need to continually update your skills to position yourself for future changes, personally and professionally. It is up to you to make this happen. Don't take on the mindset that someone else is supposed to guide you through this process. Know your desired outcome and enjoy learning!

Decisive – *having the power to decide, determined.* Making decisions involves risks. Gather as much data as you can and make the best decision you can. It may not always turn out right or the way you intended, but you made the decision. Stand by it. Make revisions when applicable and move on.

Initiative – *an introductory step.* Taking the first step can sometimes be scary because you're entering the unknown. Don't let fear stop you. Take the step to do what needs to be done when it needs to be done. Don't procrastinate.

Self-discipline – *the disciplining or controlling of oneself, of one's desires, actions, habits, etc.* You know what's right and wrong, good and bad. Act on it!

Conviction – *belief.* Decipher what this is for yourself. Unfortunately, we possess the beliefs of others without truly knowing why.

Responsible – *able to be called upon to answer for one's acts or decisions.* Knowing you've done your best makes it easy to defend your acts and decisions.

Action-oriented – *set in a position of performing.* None of this means anything if you don't take action.

Self-confidence – *confidence in oneself, one's own abilities.* Refrain from comparing yourself with others. You have your own talents and uniqueness. You have to be confident in and secure with yourself because people will try to break you, crack your foundation. They'll come at you from many angles in ways that will be petty and immature. They'll present you with negativity that is not worth your time or thoughts. Get rid of it as fast as you can and remain focused on the positive.

Respect – *to consider deserving or high regard.* If you want to be treated with respect, you must treat others with respect.

Integrity – *the quality or state of being of sound moral principle, uprighteous, honesty, and sincerity.* Maintaining integrity is a continuous effort. This should not become a tennis match to fit what you want to do at a particular time.

As a leader, you must have the ability to:

• Lead yourself (Would you follow a leader that can't lead himself/herself?).

• Think for yourself (even if you seek the advise of others).

• Be responsible and accountable.

• Look at the whole picture.

• Evaluate and analyze.

- Anticipate.

- Take action.

- Make revisions when applicable.

It's up to you to obtain what you need to be successful (based on your definition of success). Because you are part of a bigger world, don't ever think it's just you, or that it's all about you. Don't let your head swell to the point that you disregard others or think some people are inferior to you. Don't be self-centered. In addition to defining who you are, remember, you are also here to serve others.

"Do not let any unwholesome talk come out of your mouths,
but only what is helpful for building others up according to their needs,
that it may benefit those who listen."
(Ephesians 4:29)

People want to feel important and useful, they want to make a difference. People need people they can rely on. People need great leaders. It is a tough responsibility. Will you be that person?

Source:
Bible

ABOUT THE AUTHOR

Dr. Joyce Roland Ph. D. MSN

Dr. E. Joyce Roland is a doctorally prepared registered nurse with expertise in women's health from a holistic perspective (mental, physical and spiritual). She is currently an clinical associate professor of nursing at North Carolina Central University, Durham, North Carolina. She is also president and founder of The Roland Group, a service that focuses on Wellness Training, Leadership Development, Stress and Conflict Management, as well as the mental, physical and spiritual health of women. She is a teacher, writer, and researcher in mental and physical wellness for women, and especially African-American women.

Dr. Roland received a BS in Nursing from Winston-Salem State University, a masters degree in Nursing from Seton Hall University, South Orange, NJ, and a doctorate in Community Psychology from North Carolina State University, Raleigh, NC. Since 1978 she has worked as a nurse educator and research psychologist. From 1997 to 1999 she completed post-doctoral studies in Alcohol and Substance Abuse Epidemiology (as it relates to women) at the Alcohol Research Group, University of California, Berkeley (1997-99), and most recently completed research on posttraumatic stress disorder among women veterans (2004-06). She enjoys working with women and young girls, teaching them self-care and self-improvement strategies and providing mid-career advice to women.

Her most recent community work has been with a Durham-based Rites of Passage program for African-American girls and volunteering with the Urban Ministries of Durham—a community agency for the homeless—teaching life skills development for women and preparation for re-entry into society. She likes to travel and has visited Mexico, Haiti and other Caribbean Islands, and most recently traveled to England, visiting Coventry Cathedral to learn more about strategies for promoting peace and reconciliation in the world.

Dr. Roland is a member of The Professional Woman's Network, a life member of Delta Sigma Theta Sorority, and a member of N.C. League for Nurses. She is an active member of St. Paul AME Church in Chapel Hill, NC serving on the Trustee Board and the Health committee. She also sings in the choir.

She is married to her husband, Lewis, and has three adult daughters: Leslie, Kaifa, and Lisa, and two beautiful granddaughters, Cameren and Asha.

Contact:
E. Joyce Roland, RN, PhD, MSN
125 Hidden Springs Drive
Durham, NC 27703
(919) 598-1917
jaylew@intrex.net
www.protrain.net

FIVE

WAYS TO CREATE A CALM AND PEACEFUL LIFE

By Dr. E. Joyce Roland

"I lift my eyes unto the hills; where does my help come from?"
Psalms 121-The African-American Devotional Bible

A way to peace and calm…is there such a path? Do African-American women have the ability to lead a calm and peaceful life? One might ask, "How is this possible in our fast-paced, 'do unto others before they do unto you' – world?" Is such a way of life attainable? From the beginning we must understand that the answer does not lie totally within our power. The answer lies beyond us. My personal advice for the creation of a new path of 'peace and calm' is to put God first in your life and ask for assistance in designing for yourself a new life.

As African-American women, we often feel invisible, overlooked, overwhelmed, and overbooked. However, from a societal perspective, we are looked upon and often referred to as "strong black women." We hear the phrase so often we begin to believe that we must live up to this stereotype. We embrace this so deeply that it embodies the very fibers of our being. To admit to not being able to live up to this societal or self-imposed image somehow makes us appear vulnerable and weak. For many of us, we act as if we believe the myth that indeed God did pick us out and give us this special gift. And perhaps (s)he did. But how wisely are we using the gift?

Inquire of any Black woman on any given day and she will probably share with you that her life is certainly less than calm and peaceful. In truth, many Black women appear calm on the outside, but on a daily basis, live a very hectic, chaotic and unbalanced life. In most instances you will find us trying to be all things to all people. Is there a solution for this contrived existence? Is there a better way? First Corinthians 12:31 assures us that, "God will show us an even more excellent way." We have to desire a more calm and peaceful life and actively seek it.

What does it mean---to lead a calm and peaceful life? What brings us to calm? What keeps us calm? As you know it does not happen automatically. I say CALM is a learned behavior. The skills to live such a life are developed over time and with practice. We do not acquire these skills simply as a result of living a certain number of years. They often have to be learned. We do have to desire this CALM in our lives. This is probably the first step - cultivate the desire to change.

Step One: Recognize that you do want a calm and peaceful life.

When you truly decide that this is your truth, you need to take steps to achieve this state. We grow into this state of being with the knowledge that the only person we can control is our self. We must realize that, if we do not like living our lives the way we do, then we must change the things in our environment that contribute to the turmoil and upheaval in our lives. If I want to change the direction or level of upheaval in my life, I need to look very closely inside myself at what I can change, and what I want to change. I may need to whisper a prayer asking to be shown where changes can be made. I need to put God first.

Step Two: Put God first.

Putting God first leads us to the answers we seek. Developing a calm and peaceful life is a journey, and as an older African-American woman in the middle of my sixth decade on planet Earth, I've learned that achieving calm and peace is a lifetime effort and an ever-evolving process. It requires self-discipline, fortitude, and attitudinal changes. As the Bible puts it, "We must put on the whole armor of God." Simply put, this achievement has to be worked at systemically, one day at a time. What I mean by this is that for some it may take a lifetime for this self-evolution to occur. However, age is not a prerequisite. You can start at any age if you desire change.

As stated before, one must decide that she no longer enjoys or will tolerate the chaotic lifestyle. We as African-American women must decide that it makes sense to have a more calm and peaceful life. Many of us are so used to so much external stimuli (chaos) in our lives that we attempt to function in spite of it. We scatter our energy all over, then we wonder why our hair is falling out, our nerves are frayed, and we always have a never-ending list of unfinished tasks. Is there a way out of this pattern of living? I say there is. In the pages that follow I will describe some of the personal actions we as Black women can take to heal ourselves.

Step Three: Meditation, Visualization and Journaling

First, you must focus or concentrate on what it is that you want to change about your way of life. What would your life look like if it were somehow calm and peaceful? Take a moment to close your eyes and visualize this desired state of being. Take a slow deep breath and exhale v-e-r-y slowly through your pursed lips. Count to eight (1- 2- 3- 4- 5- 6- 7- 8) and exhale. Take another deep breath. Repeat this technique, breathing slowly 3 - 5 times over about five minutes. Imagine (visualize) the life you desire. What do you see? What do you envision your new life to be? What are you doing that you don't now do? What would you eliminate?

After this visualization exercise, take a few minutes and write down the thoughts that came to mind during this exercise. Write all thoughts down each time you complete a visualization exercise. When you write these ideas down, they become concrete, tangible, and more easily attainable for you. Write the images down; draw pictures, if you can. A written goal is much easier to follow and measure. As long as it is only in your head, the idea is only a supposition, proposition or wish. How do you make it a reality? The vision must come from you. Until you can visualize and articulate a new life, it remains out of your reach. How does what you visualize differ from your typical day? What changes must you make to achieve your vision?

Write it down and make it happen. You can do it!

Step Four: For Serenity's Sake - Breathe.

As described above, meditative breathing can help you begin to actualize a calm and peaceful life. Nice and easy meditative breathing can help you achieve calm. Every time you take in a breath, you bring in a fresh flow of air, which contains oxygen. Oxygen helps with metabolism and the generation of new energy. It feeds all the cells in your body. The sudden influx of oxygen ignites your brain, which is the seat of all behavior. As we breathe out old, stale air or carbon dioxide, we breathe out loads of old energy, contaminated and filled with negative thought patterns. As you breathe out, focus on clearing your head (brain) of all the negative energy you have accumulated all day. Clear it of all extraneous thought. Stay in this meditative mode for about five to fifteen minutes (even longer if time permits), and see how much better you feel when you return to the real world. <u>Stop and do it now!</u>

See how much more relaxed you feel. You can achieve this state of calm any time you desire by simply ceasing all activity and finding a quiet place to sit and engage in quiet moments.

Breathing is a divine secret. Breathing purposefully makes one take time to appreciate and discover our gifts. It helps us decide how to use our gifts. Deep breathing helps us gain more control over our environment. At the same time, it feeds our bodies at the cellular level. Our cells need fresh air (oxygen) to respond to the many demands made on our being on a daily basis.

Step Five: Create a daily ritual.

I am suggesting to you that you create a daily ritual to maintain your new calm and peaceful life. Find a place in your home that allows you to have complete peace and quiet for at least 20-30 minutes. Choose the same time and place each day, if possible, go into this space, and find your peace. This ritual can be repeated in the evening, or better still, whenever you wish. Try it for one month and notice the difference.

Step Six: Be Led By the Spirit –"Let Go and Let God".

Another important step in achieving a calm and peaceful life is to "Let Go and Let God!" When I first came upon this affirmation, I had to ponder its meaning. However, the more it rolled off my tongue, the more the message sank in. Not my will, but God's. Not my way, but God's. For me, this affirmation reminded me to "let God handle it." Let go of those things over which I have no control. Let it go. If I don't have control over it, let it go - let God handle it. This is the most difficult thing for many of us to do (myself included). But I offer you this as a daily affirmation. Get in the habit of realizing when and how to let go and see what happens. Make this a verbal affirmation when things get tough! Just say, "Let go and let God." See how much better things will turn out.

Often, as African-American women, we want to do it ourselves - our way. That may be why few things of substance seem to be realized - my way, or no way. But stop – have you talked to God about it? We have absolutely no power over the outcome of events in our lives. We plan them, set them up, but the final outcome is a result of giving it up to a higher power -letting go! After you have planned and organized and fixed and invited, it is then time to "Let Go and see how God fixes it." You'll be pleasantly surprised.

Having learned this during my fifth decade of life (my 50s), I began to function so much better. Oh, I sometime forget and think I have it all together, but some event will snatch me back to the reality that I am trying to control things. I learn and practice daily to "let go" what I can't change and leave it to God or to whatever Higher Power you subscribe. I go to my special place, put on my meditative music, and focus on manifesting calm and peace.

Step Seven: Develop your spiritual self.

Perhaps some of you may have trouble with the Christian principles of love, faith and prayer. If you have other principles you live by from other religious beliefs, by all means, use them. I believe in the development of our spiritual side, whatever it is. When we use it, we become more calm and peaceful. Twenty years ago, I could not have imagined me having the temerity to put thoughts such as these on paper. I don't even know if I considered myself a spiritual person, even though I grew up in a Christian church and home. I might have called myself a Christian, but the missing ingredients were the spirituality and the faith.

Becoming aware of yourself as a spiritual being helps lead you to the "peace and calm." As a spiritual being, you recognize your strengths and weaknesses, and you realize that you need help from others along the way. As a spiritual being, you exist in body (physical) and spirit. On the spiritual realm, you are connected to everything and everybody in the universe. You are a part of events greater than you. What I am trying to share with you is that achieving the calm and peaceful lifestyle is a journey that requires use of all our being. Achieving the calm and peaceful life comes with practice; it comes with age and maturity, and it comes with living every day to the fullest on a spiritual level. Peace and calm bring with it the recognition what you can and can't do; what you want and do not want to do, and deciding once and for all what you will and will not do.

As A (Wo)Man Thinketh

Do you realize that our thoughts about issues control our actions? If we think we cannot accomplish a task, then we won't accomplish that task. We may not even attempt it. If we focus and think positively about the events in our lives, the changes that occur will be positive, and the challenges will become attainable. Our thoughts affect our actions. Ban negative thinking!

Lastly, we must learn that we cannot be all things to all people. When we attempt to do this, we lose ourselves, and we are no good to ourselves or anyone else. In a nutshell, achieving a calm and peaceful life is probably a phenomenal undertaking that may require major overhaul of your life style. It takes focus and planning. It requires that you take charge of your life (with God leading the way). You must take back your life from all the outside and oft times negative stimuli that bombard your senses day in and day out.

Bring Order to Your Life.

Let's put it in perspective. You begin and end your day with chaos. There is no rhyme or reason for what you do. You merely do what you think you must do, and some how at the end of the day you will feel whole, complete and gratified. Is this not true? Perhaps the best way to begin your day – any day – is to plan for it the night before. What do I mean? To have order in your day you must know what lays before you on the next day. Not that you can always control events this way. But, if you get into the habit of making a list of what you need to do, preferably before going to bed, you will sleep more soundly because you have given thought to what lay before you on the next day. And by so doing, you will have cleared your mind of all those swirling thoughts that nag you and keep you tossing and turning at night. Technically, when this happens you are guilty of working while you are supposed to be resting and recovering your energy for the next day. Reclaim the time in your day. Make realistic plans for daily activities.

Some Final Thoughts –

From the beginning, I have suggested, "putting God first." What else does this mean? Ponder this – "Putting God first" means thanking God upon awakening. Be thankful for having experienced a restful night's sleep. Thank God before going to bed each night, and as many self-actualized persons have suggested, at the end of each day write down all the reasons you have to be thankful. This action, taken on a regular (daily) basis, will help you sleep soundly and help you rebound from whatever the day's activities might have wrought upon you.

Another action plan: when you can't sleep at night – get up and write down all the thoughts running through your mind. Keep pen and paper by your bedside. This is a good time to make the "to do" list for the next day, if you've not done so already. Getting this over-abundance of information out of your head and on paper will relieve your subconscious, freeing your body and mind to relax and fall asleep. You will be surprised how well you will sleep and how well you will feel on awakening the next day. It also allows for new ideas to surface from your subconscious. If you find this writing activity to be productive, take it to the next level and begin keeping a journal. Journaling has worked wonders for me in terms of sorting out the problem spots and making decisions regarding changes to make in my life.

Now is the time to do a self-assessment on where you are with your life and where you seem to be heading. This is a good time to determine if you need to put new plans in place in order to accomplish that more calm, peaceful and balanced life you are seeking. Below is a list of ideas that came up as I began to develop this recipe for a calm and peaceful life. Take a look at them. I have not covered all areas. But begin to think on these things and see how your life will change.

- Share with others.

- Do for others.

- Pray for others.

- Live in the now (mindfulness) one day at a time.

- Don't let others steal your joy.

- Begin and end each day with prayer.

- Stay tuned for the answers that will come.

- Make time for yourself.

- Write it down (Journaling).

- Live life to the fullest (one day at a time).

- Keep your temple (body) healthy.

- Be careful what you wish for.

Most of all, remember that God is Good, and God (Good) is in you. What you are seeking is already inside of you. It is your reason for being on this Earth. Use your gifts wisely and you will enjoy a CALM and PEACEFUL life. May the Peace of God go with you!

Resources :

Books:

The Purpose Driven Life. Warren, Rick (2002). Zondervan Press. Grand Rapids, Mich.

VanZant, Iyanla – All of her books and writings

The Daily Word. (A book of daily readings and affirmations). Unity Village, St. Louis, Missouri.

A Woman's Book of Life: The Biology, Psychology and Spirituality of the Feminine Life Cycle. Borysenko, Jean (1996). The Berkeley Publishing Group, New York. (New paperback edition).

Ten Secrets for Success and Inner Peace. Dyer, Wayne. (2001). Hay House, Inc. Carlsbad, CA.

Manifest Your Destiny: The Nine Spiritual Principles for Getting Everything You Want. Dyer, Wayne. (1999). Harper Paperbacks: HarperCollins Publishers, New York.

Music for Meditation: CD
Migration: Peter R. Carlos with David Darling, Mark Miller & Chris White SilverWave Records, 1992.

Sacred: by Jeff Majors, 2004.

Activities (Things to Do):
Create a meditative space (with candles, incense and meditative music).

Spend at least 30 minutes a day or more in meditation.

Let the words of your mouth be guided by the Spirit (speak only good).

Give yourself permission to <u>not</u> be perfect or the SUPER Black Woman.

Keep a journal (write in it daily).

Take time to smell the roses!

ABOUT THE AUTHOR

OLGA CARMICHAEL, RN.,C., BSN, MA, CLNC, CGP

Olga Carmichael is President and CEO of Carmichael & Associates. She holds a Masters degree in Counseling from Amberton University in Texas, is a Certified Psychotherapist, Certified Legal Nurse Consultant, Certified Group Psychotherapist, and a Registered Nurse.

Olga also has a Bachelor's degree in Nursing and Biology from Texas Woman's University, as well as two other science degrees; she has a diploma in Psychotherapy from the Dallas and American Group Psychotherapy Association. She is an Alcohol and Drug Counselor, Certified Group Psychotherapist, Forensic Nurse, Certified Professional Development Trainer and Consultant, Certified Life and Leadership Coach, Domestic Violence, Sexual Abuse/Assault Counselor, and a member of the Critical Incident Debriefing Team. Currently she is on the Advisory Board of The International Professional WomanNetwork and is a member of The Professional Woman Speaker's Bureau conducting workshops relating to women's issues and leadership skills.

Ms. Carmichael has over twenty-eight years of experience in adult and mental health nursing. Her extensive counseling expertise includes individual, group and family counseling; post-traumatic stress disorders; grief, crisis and suicide intervention; personality disorders; gender issues; dual-diagnosed population; and workplace and domestic violence. She has a diverse counseling background using an eclectic perspective. She is highly experienced in serving diverse cultures and is currently an Employee Assistance Professional Counselor in Bermuda. She has conducted numerous workshops involving stress management, dealing with grief and loss, and behavior disorders.

Ms. Carmichael is committed to bringing outstanding seminars and presentations to corporations, organizations, and individuals; she provides education regarding the importance of diverse cultures working together while maintaining the dignity and high self-esteem of each individual.

Contact:
Carmichael & Associates
8 Whaling Hill
P.O. Box SN 213
SB 03
Bermuda
(441) 541-0695
ocarmichael@eap.bm
www.protrain.net

SIX

THE ROAD TO RECOVERY: OVERCOMING SELF-DEFEATING HABITS

By Olga Craine-Carmichael

Historically, African-American women have been deemed the matriarch of our people, dating back to slavery as the "backbone" upon which many sacrifices were made. Although they have worn many labels with external shame such as sapphire, mammy or gal, their inner pride remains undaunted. African-American women display incredible strength, tenacity and limitless love and affection. In this elusive culture we are the wage earners and primary caregivers as well as the nurturer. Black women are unique, powerful, and beautiful.

They demand a self-defined classification. Because of the diversity, this chapter will interchangeably use African-American or Black in reference to the woman. While African-American women have endured years of oppression in the past, today they assume a prominent place in our culture and society. In the United States and internationally, African-American women are in:

• Leading corporations

• High ranking military positions

• Government

• Sport championships

• Literature

• Theater

• Science

• Upper management

• Business ownership

Black women have so much to offer our society, etching the world with eminence of courage and vision. Several intelligent and dedicated African-American women are Maya Angelou, Mae Jemison, Alfre Woodard, Ruby Dee and Oprah Winfrey. They are responsible for shaping our world and doing all that is possible in making the difference for a richer and better life for their counterparts.

Great demands are placed upon the African-American woman to perform and conform to other's stereotype expectations and perceptions of the "Black Woman". Black Women can be compared to a plate of spaghetti whereby, tracing their paths, you will find they touch and intersect with each other. Like spaghetti, for example, the African-American woman's life is a process, with every thought and issue in some way connecting to each other. Because of this connection, African-American women are considered:

• Multi-tasked

• Aggressive

• Strong

• Able to persevere and endure

• Unshakable

• Superwoman

• Independent

• Non-feminine

Although our female counterparts of other races and nationalities are equally significant and share like qualities, for the purpose of this chapter the focus will highlight the uniqueness of the African-American female in overcoming the habits that may be self-defeating to her.

Understanding

The African-American woman may be the most misunderstood of the female species. With so many attributes, why has society as a whole failed to appreciate the truth of her experiences and authenticity in how it feels to be an African-American female? There is very limited knowledge related to the psychology of the African-American woman. Several aspects of their lives are largely unknown, ignored and poorly understood by the wider community. The African-American woman today cannot rely on being understood, regardless of whether she is competent, intelligent or dazzling. It remains that the Black female is misunderstood in the following areas:

- Perception of the workplace

- Challenges faced as mothers or grandmothers

- Complexities of their relationships and romantic life

- Spiritual and religious practices

- Need to conform

- Role as the African-American woman

- Morality

- Pressures they live with

- Independency vs. dependency

- Friends

- Sisterhood

- Family

- Self-empowerment

- Pride

Great expectations are imposed on the African-American woman to maintain her place in society. In addition to being in contention with her female adversaries, she is faced with placating her White colleagues and African-American men, as well as other segments of the community and society on a whole.

In an effort to meet the many demands made of her relentlessly to serve and satisfy others, Black women may develop habits to accommodate the differences they encounter. For centuries the African-American woman had to be everything to everybody. Because of the variety of roles they have portrayed, African-American women define themselves by many complexities. They tend to develop habits viewed as negative to protect their lives from being dominated by a set of oppressive, stereotype myths or a subterfuge to ensure their survival in today's society. Several oppressive myths contributing to habits that may be self-defeating or destructive are:

- She cannot be beautiful or feminine if she is strong.

- If sexually harassed or accosted, she is considered oversexed or promiscuous if she postures with pride.

- If she is well-traveled, she may be accused of some illegal activity rather than just seeing the globe.

- People determine her level of intelligence by the type of work she does.

- If she is able to take care of her family, she is considered tough and unafraid.

Self-Defeating Habits

African-American women seem to have an affinity in responding to negative messages; negative messages, subsequently using it as a shield of survival. A study conducted by the African-American Women's Voice Project supported findings with reference to the Shifting Principle. Shifting is a change in behaviors used in understanding the pressures African-American women encounter and live with throughout their lives. It is similar to a learned pattern of behaviors in which the same behaviors are emulated and passed on. Shifting behaviors occurred in our ancestors and female heroes. The mental, emotional and physical compromises made by them were of utmost importance because their lives depended on it.

Exercise 1

Write down three negative traits you have encountered as an African-American female.

1. _____

2. _____

3. _____

Initially, Shifting's design was to be a positive component of the African-American woman because of the "survival device". However, over time Shifting not only became a negative habit, but subsequently it has become a defense mechanism. The intention of the Shifting was to exert a positive influence for the Black woman; however, in contrast, it provided the opposite effect. By definition, the habits are termed negative because this acquired pattern of behavior became almost involuntary, due to the frequency in repetitive behaviors. Shifting proved as a self-defeating habit because the African-American woman repeatedly disconnected from who she actually was to who she had to pretend to be. Shifting has become an integral part of the Black woman's mannerism from one moment to the next.

These self-defeating habits of Shifting can be seen in how African-American woman:

• Change their external behavior to accommodate the situation

• Change in attitude or tone from one environment to another For example:

1. Shifting to accommodate another race then back to African heritage again

2. Speaking one way at work, another way to her mother, and still a different way to her girlfriend

3. Attempting not to demonstrate an aggressive nature to her boss of another race (male or female) then shifting to deal with the African-American male counterpart in a completely different or alternate manner

4. Covering up the way she feels about herself

Shifting is the root cause of many self–defeating behaviors in the African-American woman because this is how she is viewed by society. This is the personality the Black woman has adopted, or shall we say adapted to. It is the build up of these Shifting behaviors that present problems. It is the need to satisfy this role that contributes to the negative habits. Shifting is how the African-American woman meets and greets the world. Of all groups including gays, lesbians, Latinos, Mexicans, and Native Americans, the African-American woman Shifts more than most other races or special groups.

Exercise 2

Reflect on a time when you were in a Shifting role during your normal workday.

1. What was the situation in which the Shift occurred?

_____

2. With whom did the Shift occur?

_____

3. What was the Shift?

_____

Shifting is often internal or invisible; however, it can be external and outward. Shifting today is more subtle and insidious. Shifting can be seen as negative or positive, having a direct influence on the self-defeating behaviors referred to as habits. There are positives to Shifting as it can effect how the negatives are dealt with only if the Black woman becomes aware of these habits.

The following are situations which Shifting outcomes may be negative.

1. Debra is a thirty five year old African-American single parent who identifies her negative thinking Shifting habits as having to show strength while hiding her sense of vulnerability. Because she is poorly educated, Debra feels a need to overcompensate in her role as breadwinner. This has an overwhelming negative influence for a Black woman, because now she is forced into an emotional competition against herself.

2. A single African-American woman in her fifties cites her Shift or self–defeating habits that she is too self-sacrificing and lacks the inability to say no. She has successfully produced a daughter with a Master's degree; however she finds it difficult to say no in fear of offending someone.

In discussing the meaning of self-defeating habits with other African-American women within their community, the following problems were shared:

• Many self-imposed limitations

• Self-imposed esteem issues

• Over-enmeshed or engaged

• Superwoman

• Failure to realize potential

• Self denials

• Fighting amongst ourselves

- Lack of identity

- Abandonment of true identity

- Denying physical, psychological, emotional and spiritual needs

- Envy and jealousy

- Lack of cohesion between women

- Self-serving to the African-American male

- The prevalence of using race as a crutch in under-achieving or reaching full potential

- Using the history of the African-American women as a crutch or reason for self-defeat

- Dependence on the African-American male for rescue

A colleague whom I hold in high esteem summarizes the above opinions by stating, "As African-American women, many issues must be addressed in order for our daughters to realize or embrace our great purpose and worth in this society. Actions must be implemented soon in order to lay the foundation for the present and future generation of Black woman to benefit." (Birdie Carlton).

Exercise 3

Take a moment to review the above self-defeating Shifts. What would your actions be to change the habit of:

1. Being a superwoman? _____

2. Lack of identity? _____

3. Self-denials? _____

4. Jealousy? _____

5. Envy? _____

Exercise 4

If we as African-American women face many issues in overcoming these self-defeating behaviors, (which we have developed into a habit by repetition), then what are you willing to do?

List three actions:

1. _____

2. _____

3. _____

Overcoming the Shift

The habit of Shifting for many African-American women can have positive effects. Shifting may serve as a survival or an adaptive mechanism. For example, the African-American woman explores different parts of herself through Shifting, which provides the pathway to connect with other Black women who may be very different from herself. Because Shifting allows the Black woman to secure opportunities in the social, business and educational sector, she is the representative of all other African-American women and the symbol of how they are viewed. (Of mention is the fact that women of other races who are darker skinned are challenged with the Shifting syndrome, as well.)

Another Shifting or self-defeating habit facing the African-American woman almost daily is the Lily Complex (Taking on the characteristics and behaviors of another race) This is one of the most insidious complexes, because the Black woman has to deal with the pressure of conforming to the standards of how she is being viewed by her female sisters of another race. She struggles with her outward expression, which oftentimes is not matching her inner-self. Because of her desire to meet the expectations of others, the African-American woman's psyche is altered.

The African-American woman possesses the qualities needed in meeting adversities she encounters. Some of these women may use the Lily Complex to help them integrate into the mainstream to gain certain or specific opportunities. However, these Black women have not given up nor deserted their identity. They make claims to the uniqueness of their blackness. Another instance in which the Lily Complex takes a strange twist and may prevent a woman from connecting with her full blackness is turning against another African-American sister. This habit is usually out of frustration by trying to live up to others expectations.

Although these aspects historically have presented barriers for the African-American woman who has now become comfortable with being acknowledged as an African to denote her race, the Black woman overcomes the self–defeating behaviors by:

• Owning her Blackness

• Her outward Shifting complementing her inner-self

• Accepting her beauty

• Individualizing her representation of her blackness

- Believing in herself

- Believing she is worthy

- Letting go of enmeshments

- Exerting her independence

- Putting herself first

- Stop comprising herself physically, mentally and emotionally

- Satisfying self expectations

- Defining herself and her Blackness

- Staying with her Blackness in situation that she shifted in the past

- Using support and encouragement instead of jealousy and envy

Exercise 5

You have just been made partner in a large firm and there are several other African-American women who will answer to you. You recently decided to define who you are and assert your Blackness. Identify three choices from the above Shifts as to how you will behave:

1. _____

2. _____

3. _____

Exercise 6

How would you deal with other African-American women?

1. _____

2. _____

3. _____

The African-American woman possesses the traits for surviving in society today. Although she had to fight and struggle for her place in this society (and among other cultures), there is uniqueness within her demanding attention. With her beauty, strength and endurance she can define who she is and demand her status. The many great African-American women who have fought to remove stigma of these negative behaviors have paved the way for us to move forward. In order for us to move forward, the shift has to be used in a positive and constructive manner. To use the Shifts in recovering from these self-defeating habits, the Black woman will reclaim her Shifts, using them to define who she is and her purpose. The positive Shift is the cross over into the future.

Recommended Reading

Men Are Like Waffles: Women Are Like Spaghetti Farrel B. & Farrel P. (2001). Oregon: Harvest House Publishers

Shifting: The Double Lives Of Black Women in America. Jones & Shorter-Gooden, K. (2003). New York: Harper Collins

For Black Women Only. Hicks, E.D. (1991). Illinois: African-American Images.

Notes:

_____

_____

_____

_____

_____

_____

_____

_____

_____

_____

_____

_____

_____

_____

_____

_____

_____

_____

_____

_____

_____

_____

ABOUT THE AUTHOR

NOTHRICE ALFORD

Nothrice Alford, ED. S. received her undergraduate degree in Elementary Education from Albany State University, her Master Degree from Georgia State University and her Education Specialist Degree from Troy State University. She was certified as a Reading Recovery Teacher at Georgia State University. She is listed in the 2006 edition of Who's Who Among American Teachers. She is currently a reading teacher in Atlanta, Georgia. She has one daughter, Kia, a graduate student in Florida A&M University.

Ms. Alford is the CEO and President of The Heritage Institute for Personal Excellence, a coaching and training consulting organization. She is a member of The Professional Woman Network (PWN). She was recently named to The Professional Woman Network International Advisory Board for 2006-2007.

She is certified Training Consultant in the areas of Cultural Diversity, Stress Management, Customer Service and Professionalism. She's also a Certified Life Success Coach.

Ms. Alford is a contributing author in, A Train Runs Through It, a book of stories and memories about her hometown. She is also a contributing author for *Survival Skills for the African-American Woman* and the forthcoming *Women as Leaders: Strategies for Empowerment & Communication*.

Nothrice Alford is available for presentations, seminars, workshops, consultation, and coaching on a regional, national, and international basis.

Contact:
The Heritage Institute of Personal Excellence
P.O. Box 40
Mableton, GA 30126
nothrice@bellsouth.net
www.protrain.net

SEVEN

COUNT YOUR BLESSINGS: A LESSON IN POSITIVE ATTITUDE

By Nothrice Alford

You are blessed with the gift of life. Having a positive attitude about life will increase your blessing. Counting your blessings is as simple as just "saying thank you", no matter the circumstances. Webster Dictionary defines blessings as a short prayer before a meal, and it defines bless as to honor and praise. In the Revealing Word, a dictionary of Metaphysical Terms, it states that blessing imparts the quickening spiritual power that produces growth and increase. It is the power of multiplication. It defines bless as to confer God's good on something or someone.

Be optimistic about life and know what is true for you. It helps to have a positive attitude for you set the tone for what you will receive. A positive attitude will change your self-image. Keeping a gratitude journal will allow you to reflect on your life and appreciate the abundance you have. By following the steps of "saying thank you," being optimistic about life, having a positive mental attitude and keeping a gratitude journal, you set in motion the law of increase. What you dwell on will increase. Gratitude is an attitude. Your attitude is your life.

Say Thank You

We often take for granted the very things that most deserve our gratitude. Begin by giving thanks for the small things. Start discipling yourself to be thankful for tiny bits and then build your way up to being thankful for more. The more thankful you become, the more good will flow into your life. Stop complaining about the past or your present condition. Give thanks, no matter what your past or present circumstances may be.

Meister Eckhart stated, "If the only prayer you ever say in your whole life is 'Thank you', that would suffice." Everything that happens is an opportunity for growth and an opportunity to say "thank you." Give praise and thanks in everything.

Talk show host, Oprah Winfrey, stated in an article that saying the words "thank you" turned her life around. One day about ten years ago, she was on the phone with her friend and mentor Maya Angelou. Oprah was sitting in her bathroom with the door closed and the toilet lid down, and was booing and ahooing on the phone so uncontrollably that she was incoherent. "Stop it! Stop it right now! And say thank you!" Maya chided. "But – you don't understand." Oprah sobbed. To this day, Oprah can remember what it was that had her so far gone, which only proves the point Maya was trying to make. "I do understand," she told Oprah. "I want to hear you say it now. Out loud. "Thank you."

Tentatively, Oprah repeated it: "Thank you - but what am I saying it for?"

"You are saying thank you," Maya said, "because your faith is so strong that you don't doubt that whatever the problem, you'll get through it."

Self-Reflection

Count your blessings. List things that you have taken for granted in the past.

1. _____
2. _____
3. _____
4. _____
5. _____

Give thanks for the infinite abundance of God. Appreciate the blessings you have and be open and receptive to the new ones as they come into your life. Stop talking about limitations, and see the blessings only. Stop complaining and give thanks. Try to go through one whole day saying "thank you" to everything and everyone who does something that serves you in anyway. No matter how you are feeling, you should give thanks. Thank God for guiding you through life thus far and for guiding you in the days to come.

Optimism

Focus on the good in your life. Focus on the good you desire to manifest in your life. What you focus on you will receive. Always focus on the objective, not the obstacle.

F - Face reality. (or **F**ocus on God).

O – Optimistic (or **O**rganize your thoughts)

C - Concentrate on your desired outcome. (or **C**ommit yourself).

U - Unite with positive people. (or **U**nderstand your purpose).

S - See your desire for what it is. (or **S**tay centered).

Start your day by putting God first. God is the source of all blessings. Focus your attention on God, away from the outer distractions. When you focus on the spirit of God within, you will be blessed with success in every area of life. We are creations of God who are blessed in all that we do. With a vision, you set the tone for the blessings that are possible for you. A challenge can be easily turned into an opportunity to see a larger vision for ourselves.

Optimistic people see opportunities. Always focus on the objective, not the obstacle.

Obstacles are what you see when you take your eyes off your objective. Speak out your expectation by giving thanks in advance. When you pray, expect and accept your blessings as if you have already received it. Every failure is a stepping stone to success when you have a positive attitude. Every mistake is a stepping stone to success.

Before you begin each day, before going out, speak your expectations. Remember that life and death is in the power of the tongue. Speak the life you desire into your present situation. It's not enough to just believe, you have to speak it into existence. Practice using affirmations. Affirmations are positive statements of truth. They give power to your desires until they become a reality.

Keep your hopes up. Believe in yourself. Have faith in your abilities. You are equipped with everything you need to succeed. As you believe, so shall you receive. Believing in yourself means never giving up. Never let yourself get down. Giving up is not an option.

Make a decision that you want to go to the next level. Look for the blessing in every situation. Expect a blessing. Expect good things to happen. Know that all things are working together for your good.

Positive Attitude

When you are positive and enthusiastic, good thing will happen to you. Concentrate on finding whatever is good in every situation. Seek to find the good in everything, always. Whatever is going on around you is suppose to be. There is a lesson to learn from every experience you have. Learn the lesson and you will receive the blessing. If you don't learn the lesson, you will repeat the class.

Evaluate your present attitude. If you change your attitude, you will improve your life. Commit to change your attitude. Become someone with a positive mental attitude. High thoughts make you feel good and low thoughts make you feel bad. Awareness is the beginning of change.

Cassandra Walker Simmons, author of *Becoming Myself,* states in her introduction that anytime someone says something to her that she finds offensive or hurtful, she digs down inside and remembers the good things. Now she looks in the mirror and says:

> *If I believe in myself, I can do.*
> *If I believe in myself, there's no stopping me.*
> *If I believe in myself, I know I can win.*
> *Believing in myself is where it all begins.*

At the elementary school where I work in Atlanta, Georgia the students adopted this statement as their "pledge to myself". During the morning announcement each day the students recite this "pledge to myself", after the pledge of allegiance. This sets the tone for the day. It gives the student a positive outlook for what they can accomplish. The students have used this pledge for more than ten years. The student meets and/or exceeds goals and scores high on standardized test as well. Believe in yourself!

All blessings originate from God. Be open and receptive to the blessings of God. By having a positive attitude, you will continue to be blessed. Your positive attitude about life will greatly influence your outcome in life. Set your expectations by what you know to be your truth. People don't get what they want in life, they get what they expect. When you stay positive, good things will happen to you. Live the truth of your identity.

Everything is based on faith. Faith is activated when you start believing. You must set God's power in motion and give it direction. In order for God's power to work for us, it must work through us. God in us is the fountain out of which springs all our good. Having a positive mental attitude is vital to your well being. We live in a mental atmosphere - it sucks up every thought. Be careful about what you are thinking.

Four Steps to a Positive Attitude

1. Read books about positive thinking.

2. Listen to positive thinking tapes.

3. Associate with positive people.

4. Connect with a spiritual center.

The greatest people in the world read positive thinking books, listen to positive thinking tapes and associate with positive thinking people. They also have positive affirmations posted in their home and work place. Only do that which will put positive thoughts, positive images, positive ideas, positive things and positive people in your life. Surround yourself with people who believe in you and encourage you. Read positive thinking books. Invest in yourself and purchase positive thinking tapes and books. You will be inspired by the positive things you read, and listen to, on a regular basis.

Gratitude Journal

Establish a definite time to journal each day. Be consistent with your schedule for journaling. Make a decision to write in your journal each morning upon arising or each night before going to bed. Write at least five things that you are grateful for. Writing crystallizes your thoughts. Be grateful no matter what is going on in your life. Whatever you give your attention to you create more of the same. Take nothing for granted and show gratitude for every gesture of kindness. Be thankful for the luxury of life and the gift of love. Nothing is more honorable than to have a grateful heart. Begin each day with gratitude.

Self-Reflection

List 5 things that you are grateful for upon waking up each the morning.

1. _____

2. _____

3. _____

4. _____

5. _____

Give thanks for the lessons in your life. There is a blessing in every lesson. If you lose the lesson, no one else will get the blessings. God blesses us with life! Each day is a new beginning to a fresh start. Each day God give us the opportunity to count our blessings. Every day is an opportunity to be grateful for the things we have. You are blessed by the abundance all around you - food to eat, a place to call home, and clothing to wear. Be grateful to be a conduit of God's joy in your home and work place, in your neighborhood, and the world. The people you meet are blessed by the joy that rises up within you and overflows from you.

Each night before going to bed, gently release each day with appreciation for how abundantly blessed you truly are. To cultivate gratitude you need to develop a new habit of attention. Spend some time each day in self-reflection. Though self-reflection, we can come to see everything we have and are, as gifts of God. Through self-reflections we begin to train our attention to notice what we haven't noticed before. Ultimately, self-reflection offers us a chance at transforming ourselves, and our relationship with others.

Self-Reflection
List 5 things that you are grateful for before going to bed each night.
1. _____
2. _____
3. _____
4. _____
5. _____

In a quote taken from the 35th President of the United States John Fitzgerald Kennedy, he states, "*As we express our gratitude, we must never forget that the highest appreciation is not to utter words, but to live by them."* We give thanks to God by saying grace before meals. How often do you give thanks to people, animals, and objects around you? Utter blessings and your appreciation to everything and to everyone you encounter. By blessing others, you are blessed. Gratitude is a great mind magnet.

Each day is a fresh opportunity to be blessed and be a blessing to others. It is not just a day of the week or a date in the month - it is twenty-four hours of a greater opportunity. Make a decision that you will count your blessings in all situations that you encounter. Make a decision that you will keep a positive mental attitude always. When you choose your action, you create the consequences. Your words are setting the direction for your life.

A positive attitude draws the good. A negative attitude brings sickness, poverty and death. The world needs you to be who you are and to have a positive mental attitude. As you count your blessings, remember to be a blessing to others. You are here to enrich the place where you are. The world is counting on you to make a difference. It is not a coincidence that you are here on Earth at this time. I wish for you all the blessings in life.

ABOUT THE AUTHOR

REV. DR. MICHAEL JACKSON

Rev. Dr. Michael Jackson is the Senior Pastor and Founder of New Covenant Community Fellowship in Durham, North Carolina.

He has Bachelors degrees in Business Administration and Organizational Management, a Master of Divinity (M. Div) degree, and a Doctor of Ministry (D. Min) degree.

He received his Clinical Pastoral Education and served as Chaplain at the Veterans Administration Medical Center. He also served as a Statewide Visitor for African-American Community Outreach Program, Bryan Alzheimer's Disease Research Center, Duke Medical Center.

He is a member of the American Association of Christian Counselors (AACC), the Black African-American Christian Counselors (BAACC), the Marriage and Family Network (AACC) and he is a certified Christian Marriage and Family Therapist.

He is a member of the Fellowship of Inner-City Word of Faith Ministries (FICWFM), the 100 Black Men of America, Inc., and Professional Woman Network (PWN) and the Professional Woman Speakers Bureau and he is a Veteran of the U.S. Armed Forces.

He is married to Natalia Fisher-Jackson and has two daughters Michelle and Syreeta.

Contact:
New Covenant Community Fellowship
P.O. Box 12125
Durham, NC 27709
Phone number: 919-286-9211
Email Address: newcoveant@nc.rr.com
Website: www.empowerment4life.org

EIGHT

UNDERSTANDING THE AFRICAN-AMERICAN MALE

By Rev. Dr. Michael Jackson, D. Min

When I was first presented with this topic, I was overwhelmed by its complex magnitude. This topic can be viewed, discussed, and analyzed from so many different perspectives. It can be approached from the social, historical, racial, economical and psychological. I could write on this topic from all of these perspectives, however, it would take more than a chapter to adequately address these issues in its proper context.

As a speaker, I am constantly asked to talk on the topic of the African-American male. I am a member of two national organizations that seek to improve and enhance the quality of life of men to become better roles models and productive members of society.

I have spoken in prisons to men who have made wrong choices in life, to help them prepare to become a productive contributor to society, upon release from incarceration. However, the area that I have been approached and challenged to talk about the most is understanding the African-American male in the area of relationships.

As a Pastor and Marriage Counselor, I am approached by women who ask me the questions, "Why? Why do men cheat? Why won't men commit to a long-term relationship? Where are all the good men?" And the list goes on and on.

My objective in this chapter is not to specifically address the reasons why the man in your life did or did not do a particular thing (because I don't know the details of your specific situation), but to help the reader of this chapter gain insight into some possible causes that may contribute to those behaviors, and to help you better understand the influences that you have as a wife and a friend, in the life of the African-American male in your life.

First of all, let me start out by saying that I'm not going to be an apologist for African-American males who have been behaving badly. There are all kinds of excuses and rationalizations that can be made to try to justify certain behaviors in the lives of African-American men. Some are valid, some are not. I'm not here to defend their behavior right, wrong or indifferent, but to help you to better understand the African-American male in your life, so that you can help him be the man that you need him to be in your life.

What Do Men Want?

A common question that I get all the time is, "What do men want? I'm trying to understand him, but I just don't know what he wants!" Again, I don't know specifically what your man wants (a good idea would be to talk with him and ask him), but generally speaking, the one thing I have found that every African-American male needs and desires is: **Respect.**

Every African-American male has a need to be respected, appreciated, and valued. He has a need to feel like a King. Not in the sense that he desires to lord over or rule, but to occupy that special place in his home that gives him meaning and purpose in life. In society, the African-American male yearns for respect. He feels that no matter what he does or doesn't do, he is not respected.

Whatever he accomplishes in life is never enough. He feels disrespected in society, disrespected at work, and disrespected at home. He feels like Rodney Dangerfield, "I can't get any respect." When competing for a job, he feels like the odd man out. Even though he meets all of the criteria for the job both experientially and educationally, he still feels like the odd man out. In his mind society is against him. He feels he will not be judged by the content of his character, but he will always be judged by the stereotypical views held by society.

In his mind he feels that no matter how hard he works to better improve himself, his efforts will go unnoticed. As a result, bitterness and resentment builds, with no positive outlet. Someone needs to encourage this man. His woman needs to tell him, no matter what society may say, that he is a special part of her life, and that together they will overcome this temporary obstacle in their life.

Someone needs to help him find that enterpernual spirit on the inside of him that says if there is not an opportunity, he'll create one. Someone needs to help him tap into that spirit of determination that says, I can do - will do! So the first step in helping you understand the African-American male in your life is to show him respect by appreciating and valuing him as a man, a husband, and a friend. Help build him up, not tear him down.

I can hear someone saying, you don't know what I have to deal with, I've got my hands full. I hear you and understand your dilemma. I never said that it would be easy, however, it will be worth it in the long run. Any relationship worth having is worth working for. You have a precious raw diamond that needs the rough edges chiseled a little bit. What are you willing to invest into your relationship? You have an opportunity to help your man to be the man that you need him to be in your life.

I still hear someone in the background saying, "If I have to do all that, I will just trade him in on another model!" Let me share a secret with you, **there are no perfect men in this world**! Every man is flawed! We all have some issues going on in our lives. Let me tell you another secret, you have flaws too.

Oftentimes when I counsel couples, I share with them that they are marrying an imperfect person. At first they are taken aback by that statement, because they had a fairy tale image of skipping through a bed of flowers with a perfect mate forever. Then reality sets in and they realize that this person that they are committing the rest of their life to is not perfect. But they are human. So even if you trade him in for another model, that model will be imperfect and you may have exchanged a problem for more problems. If you respect and value the African-American male in your life, the return on your investment will be immeasurable.

He Needs Admiration.

The second step in helping you understand the African-American male in your life is that every man wants the woman in his life to be proud of him. He desires admiration. African-American males for the most part are proud individuals. We accept the mantle that has been passed down from our forefathers to be the head of the household, to be the providers of the home, to protect our children.

Unfortunately, this is not the case in every household. Therefore, the women had to step up and function as the man and the woman of the house. Women have learned to manage the household well, however, when a real man comes along there is a hesitancy to allow him to fully accept his position of leader and provider in the home. This is understandable; however, a man must be given a platform to be a man. He wants to be a good husband, he wants to be a good dad (a real man, that is) and he needs for you to affirm these qualities. Men, who feel good about themselves as the provider in the home, have more emotional resources to build upon in relationships.

When a woman tells her man that he is an excellent provider, an excellent father, and an excellent husband, those words can inspire him to achieve greater things in his life.

He sees himself doing things and he feels that he can accomplish anything, because he has the support of the woman in his life. He sees life now in a whole new way, because he feels wanted, needed, appreciated and valued as a man. Women have the power to inspire and motivate the African-American male in their lives. When a woman tells her man that she appreciates him for what he has done, it gives him more satisfaction than winning the lottery. There is power in the words that you speak.

For some men with fragile self-images, admiration helps him believe in himself. A man needs the woman in his life to be his biggest cheerleader. He draws strength and confidence from her support and encouragement. The second step in helping you understand the needs of the African-American male in your life is to provide your man with support, encouragement, and admiration.

Why Aren't Men Committed?

The third step in understanding the African-American male is in the area of commitment. The number one question that I am asked is, why are men afraid to commit in relationships?

Again, I don't know the specifics of your particular situation; however, let me offer you this bit of information to help you. I believe that men and women understand the word commitment differently. When women think of commitment, they usually think of the emotional investment in their relationship with a man. Commitment in this context involves intimacy and emotional closeness. Most women desire an emotionally invested partner in their relationship with a man. Men however, understand commitment as a sense of duty. In a man's world he is the provider, the protector of the household. For the most part his commitment is not based on emotional closeness but in economic security. Therefore, if he is committed to the relationship, he is committed from a sense of duty and obligation and not emotion. This is not to say that he is not emotionally connected to his mate. However, he is more connected to his sense of responsibility and security, and in this sense he is committed to the relationship. Unfortunately, most men that women encounter are neither emotionally, economically, nor responsibly committed to anything. Most men's problem with commitment stems from the following areas:

- social upbringing

- lack of emotional role models

- fear of being rejected and hurt

<u>Social Upbringing</u> – men are taught at an early age not to show emotions. We are taught to hide and conceal our emotions. We were taught that showing our emotions is a sign of weakness. Therefore, some men tend to not commit because in their view it is a sign of weakness. Another problem that permeates our culture as an African-American male is the mindset of "I cannot commit because it will diminish the power I have as a man". The issue is, if I commit then I no longer have leverage over my mate. Another social issue is that commitment means no more freedom. "I'm tied down. I can't go where I want to go and do what I want to do." These social views are prevalent in the African-American culture and help shape the man's view of commitment.

<u>Lack of an Emotional Role Model</u> – Another social view in the African-American culture is the lack of an emotional role model. For some men every man that they have known has been a "Playa" or a "Rolling Stone". The Father (if he was around) was a rolling stone, Granddaddy was a rolling stone, and the uncle was a rolling stone. They all have children by different mothers. There is no emotional role model for them to see or emulate. And if they do see a man in a committed relationship, it is the exception, not the norm.

<u>Fear of Rejection and Hurt</u> – Some men were in a committed relationship, but the relationship ended on a sour note. They felt hurt and rejected, therefore, in their mind they will never allow themselves to be hurt or rejected again. This is why they will enter into a relationship emotionally unattached or they will remain in the relationship until it becomes "emotional" and then they are out the door. Women don't quite know or understand what happened to change his behavior. One minute everything was all right, and then the next minute he was gone.

Women in relationships are emotionally committed, whereas, men are less emotional for fear of hurt or rejection. When men start to have feelings, it is a scary proposition. They have a problem interpreting these feelings. Some men can handle getting in touch with their feelings and commit; some men are scared and run. Communication is the key to interpreting our feelings. But most men can't talk about their feelings, especially to women. That is why they will talk to Bubba, Leroy, and June Bug in the streets and get all kinds of "manly advice" on how to handle the situation, and they are fed all kinds of "street knowledge" on feelings and relationships.

Most women tell me that they are looking for a good African-American male, however, they settled for an immature boy – parading as a man. They tell me they are looking for a BMW – a Black Man who's Working or a BME - a Black Man with an Education or a BMF – a Black Man who is Faithful, however, they settle for the opposite, a BNW – a Black Man not Working or a BNE – a Black Man with no Education or a BMU – a Black Man who is Unfaithful.

Yet they ask me where are all the good men? The question should be, why do you settle for these types of men? Why do these type of men continually gravitate towards you? How do these men move into your life and you didn't even see the moving van?

Let me offer you these words of wisdom, "If you keep going to the garbage dump, you are going to find garbage." If you keep going to the garbage dump, you are not going to find a BMW, or a BME, or a BMF, you are going to find garbage! So check out how these uncommitted men keep entering into your life. You have the key. You can keep them out or let them in. You are in control; you have the power!

If you see a pattern (club, club, club), stay out of the clubs. If you see a pattern (thug, thug, thug), look for a man with a kinder, gentler demeanor. If you see a pattern (pretty boy/ mama's boy), remember, you can take them out of the garbage dump, but they still have a garbage dump mindset that will not enhance your life, no matter how they look on the outside. A great philosopher once said, "Insanity is doing the same things, the same way, and expecting a different result." That means, if you want to stop attracting uncommitted men into your life, you have the power to do so. Make a different choice.

Men of Character

The one ingredient that all these men we've been discussing have in common is a lack of character. Character is something that is measured on the inside. It is that internal strength that says, "I won't do it, even though I want to do it." Character is what separates the men from the boys. For the most part, a lot of women have been dealing with boys instead of men. Character is what will allow the African-American male in your life to be a committed, faithful husband and father. You don't have to worry about a man of character cheating on you or abusing you and your children.

A man of character will be where he says he is going to be and will do what he says he is going to do. He is dependable. A man of character's reputation precedes him. He has a steady history of achievements and successes. A man of character helps other men to become men of character. He mentors other men and young boys. He is involved socially in the community. So stop looking for things external in a man and start looking for those internal qualities. Those external things will pass with time, but the internal qualities will last forever.

Conclusion

What I have attempted to do in this chapter is to give you some insight into understanding the African-American male in your life. I have shared with you two main things men want: **respect** and **admiration**. I have talked about commitment and I have shared with you about what not to look for in a man. I now want to leave you with these words: You have the power to choose! Don't be influenced by the pressures of society. Don't worry about some fictitious biological clock. Don't worry about the fact that you are in your mid- thirties and are unattached. Don't feel pressured by family members at reunions who don't understand why you "still" aren't married yet. Don't let these external pressures force you into making hasty decisions that you will regret the rest of your life. As a father of two daughters, I share with them that they don't need a man to be complete. Regardless of what you see in the movies or hear on the radio, you don't need a man to make you whole.

To be successful, all relationships require two whole people, not two halves. Forget the cliché that says relationships are 50/50. You have to reject that statement. In order for a relationship to work, it requires 100% commitment from both parties. You have the power to choose. Although relationships require 100%, the fact remains that no one is perfect. So in any relationship that you become involved in, know that you are involved with an imperfect person. Now, this doesn't mean that you just accept any man with two legs, but it does mean that you have the power to choose. You choose how much of this person's imperfections you want to deal with. You choose if you want to be involved with a womanizer or a man who is committed to the relationship. Again, it is your choice. Don't choose out of desperation, but choose out of prayerful consideration.

The last thing I want to share with you on this topic of understanding the African-American male is that **you have the power to influence**. From the beginning of time we see the power of a woman's influence. It began in the garden. Eve influenced Adam to do what he knew he should not have done. Women have the power to influence men both negatively or positively; you have the power to encourage the African-American male in your life. You have the power to help him find a purpose and direction in his life. You have the power to help build him up and not tear him down.

You have the opportunity to take that raw diamond and chisel him into the man that you need for him to be. You have the power. Show the African-American male in your life admiration. Let him know that you are proud of the things he has accomplished. Let him know that he is a good provider (even if you make more money than he). Let him know that he is a good father and a great husband (even though he still can improve in certain areas). Affirm the good things that he does; he needs to hear that daily. Let him know that he is not alone, but that you are with him through the good times as well as the bad.

Value and appreciate the internal qualities that he brings to the relationship. Seek out a man of character. His character will take him places that money or status can never take him.

Women, you have the power to change the destiny of the African-American male in your life. When he sees the genuine love, admiration and respect that you have for him, there is nothing that he won't do for you. In understanding the African-American male, remember that you have the power to influence him to be the man that you need for him to be in your life.

ABOUT THE AUTHOR

KAREN KYLE

Karen Kyle was born in Akron, Ohio, the last of four children. She began her studies at the University of Akron in education.

Becoming a single parent to her two year old daughter prompted her return to the University of Akron to complete her education; she later graduated with a Bachelors degree in Nursing. She began her employment at the Akron Health Department as a Public Health Nurse in Maternal Child Health, later transferring to the Adult Clinic. During her eleven years of employment at the Akron Health Department, she developed the Adult Health Diabetes Program, which provided medication, supplies, teaching, and referrals for uninsured diabetic patients. She was also Co-coordinator of the Hypertension Program.

Karen Kyle is a member of the American Diabetes Association, The Professional Woman Network, a Certified Diversity Trainer with special emphasis in women's issues, and a Nikken Independent Wellness Consultant. She is Administrative Executive for Terilyn K. Design Ltd. and listed in Manchester's Registry of Who's Who 2005-2006.

Karen is author of Soles Together, a community walking program and co-author of The Professional Woman Network book, *Self-Esteem & Empowerment for Women.*

She is currently working on a program for diabetic patients and healthcare providers at the University of Texas M D Anderson Cancer Center in the new Endocrine Outpatient Clinic that will focus on patient care, patient education, and patient responsibilities. The program will also encompass the healthcare provider's responsibilities and diversity.

Karen recently relocated to Houston, Texas, where she is employed as a registered nurse.

Contact:
Karen L. Kyle
12 Brighton Ct.
Missouri City, TX 77459
(330) 687-1308
Klkyle55@hotmail.com
www.protrain.net

NINE

PARENTING SKILLS FOR THE SINGLE WOMAN

By Karen L. Kyle

Can you remember the "good old days" playing house with your best girlfriends and your baby dolls? Every once in a while you might have gotten one or two boys into playing along and being the husbands. The girls would stay home, take care of the kids, do the housework and make mud pies for supper, while the boys would have to go to work.

You never knew what type of work they did, where they went to work or if they went. Sometimes they would leave and disappear because they didn't want to play anyway. Sometimes they got tired of playing, just disappeared and wouldn't let you know. Other times they would meet up with some of their friends and run off and play with them. You didn't realize it at that time, but you had just become a single-parent. Things haven't change very much, even in adulthood! How scary is that?

But single-parenting was never talked about; it was an embarrassment to the families. Back then divorce rates were low, mainly because the money wasn't there to pay for one. Parents just stuck it out because it was the right thing to do or there were no other choices. Women would look the other way when their husbands strayed. How much of a choice did they have with little education and no job experience? And unexpected death of a husband is a possibility no matter what era you're born.

Now women can, and do, decide to become single-parents. Your life changes as soon as that pregnancy test result is positive, or a child becomes available for adoption or if you are raising another family member's child. But understand, the rules don't change; you have a responsibility to that child, whether you are put into single-parenthood by something beyond your control or you've made a conscience decision to raise a child alone. Your life will change.

You've become not only a parent, but also a teacher, counselor, mediator, leader, cook, nurse, taxi driver and a role model, among other things. You must wear many hats; your time is shared along with your space, money, food and future.

Babies turn into toddlers, adolescents, and then adults. It would be of benefit to you as a parent to guide them to and through those stages, to make it as smooth as possible for you and your child. But raising a child is never smooth or easy. If you're making the decision to become a single-parent, know some things about yourself before you make that decision.

Know your:

- LIMITATIONS

- EXPECTATIONS

- FUTURE GOALS

- NEEDS

- WANTS

- COPING ABILITIES

- PATIENCE LEVEL

No matter how independent you are or would like to be, everyone needs a friend or a family member they feel close to when times get difficult. You need a support system, whether you're a parent or not. Raising a child alone is not impossible, but it can be one of the most challenging decisions that you'll ever make. It can also be one of the most rewarding experiences in your life. Take it from my experience, it's not easy and it can be scary at times. You'll find that you may have to do some growing up of your own.

You're no longer number one, but you must make time for yourself. Find the time to relax, renew, and unwind. These are necessities in order to continue on for yourself and your child. Having a child does not mean that you no longer exist. Taking time for yourself mentally and physically will not only increase your quality of life, but also the quantity of your life.

You should continue on with the activities that you enjoyed before becoming a parent. You will need to make changes to the schedule you had in the past, but it can be done. Other activities may need to be put on hold until your child is older. Just as you need to socialize, so does your child.

Socialization is an important part of a child's life. Interaction with other children, engaging in activities such as sports, or becoming involved with organizations/programs that will teach them new skills is essential to their growth. Introduce them to music, books, movies, church, camping, swimming or art just to name a few. You can find many activities for a child to be involved in that are offered near your home/schools. Take the time and make the effort to find them. Don't mistake their involvement of activities as a babysitting service. If parents are encouraged to participate or to be spectators, then by all means be there. Enjoy their moments of growth, as these special times only come along once.

There's nothing wrong with a babysitter or using a day care (as costly as they can be) as you may not have a choice. But before you choose either one, check them out thoroughly. Compare different day care centers, go in and ask for a tour through the facility so you can see the employees interacting with the children, and how clean the facility is kept. Each center should have a set schedule for each age group. Ask how many children to each employee, if they trained in CPR, and also inquire about being able to visit at anytime while your child is there.

If you need to hire a babysitter, don't hire a sitter based on someone else's experience with them. Talk with the person you're thinking about leaving your child with. How long have they been babysitting, have they had CPR training? Assess their maturity level, and introduce yourself to their parents. Know who you are dealing with! Your child relies on you to keep them safe, even when you can't be there. You will find that your responsibilities are 24/7, whether you're physically present or not.

Look around; notice the actions and attitudes of some of the adolescents that are "hanging out" with their friends. You can see and hear it at the malls, on the streets, on the television, in the music they listen to, and you wonder sometimes how we got to this point. You're watching learned behavior, peer pressure, and you're watching a lack of guidance. If you have teenagers, be aware of who their friends are. If you are hiring a teen babysitter for your child, learn all that you can about the babysitter.

Not only does your child need guidance from you, he/she will need guidance from their father/male in their lives. No matter the situation between you and your child's father, he needs to be a part of his child's life, if at all possible. You may feel the father is someone to keep out of your child's life, but remember there may have been a time when you thought differently. When it comes to what's best for your child, sometimes you will need to put your personal feelings aside. (If your child's father is a TRUE threat to the child, then certainly shelter them from this individual). If your child's father is truly interested in being involved with his daughter or son, learn to let go of your personal anger toward him. If you don't, this will end up poisoning your child's mind. A child needs a daddy.

It's impossible to keep everything that you consider unacceptable from your child. You, as a parent, have to explain what is right and what is wrong. You may allow your child to watch music and game videos, but you have to education that child by explaining what they are watching/listening to is entertainment, such as it is, and not at all acceptable behavior. (You may wish to monitor the video games he or she is playing, as some games are VERY violent.)

Don't expect that by sending a child to school, they will be taught everything there is to know. Our country's school system is another story. They can only teach so much and it's usually just the basics.

When you are raising a teenager, you're up against peer pressure now and that's an all-together different ballgame! Just when you thought you would be able to loosen your grip, think again. As an infant, their physical well-being was most important; now it's time to protect them mentally.

Ultimately, some of the most important parts of their education will be best learned from you. You are responsible for teaching your child:

• RESPECT/SELF-RESPECT

• TRUSTWORTHINESS

• HONESTY

• LOVE

• CARING

• RESPONSIBILITY/COMMITMENT

• SEX/RELATIONSHIPS

The more a child sees, learns, hears, touches, tastes and smells the better. Positive examples will create a positive curiosity. They will want to see, do and accomplish as much as they possibly can. They will know that there is a world outside of their own neighborhood. They will not only understand the importance of growing healthy mentally, but physically as well. Once a solid and positive foundation for learning has been started, it will continue on for the rest of their lives.

But you can hinder any growing potential for the rest of their lives too, if you're not careful. You can say or do things that you may not mean at the time, but will affect them well into adulthood. From your own experiences growing up, you were probably told, "You just don't listen!" But you were listening, and you remember what was said, even to this day. It wasn't assumed parents didn't mean what they said or did; it wasn't assumed they were "just teasing." You remember their words to this day.

What you say to a child or how you treat a child can and will effect their:

- SELF-ESTEEM

- ABILITY TO LOVE THEMSELVES AND OTHERS

- SELF-CONFIDENCE

- SELF-WORTH

- OUTLOOK

- MENTAL/PHYSICAL GROWTH

- PARENTING SKILLS

- FINANCIAL STATUS

- FUTURE

Besides, they don't need to hear criticism from you; they can get more than an ear full from their peers. That's where you come in; you're the buffer/filter between them and the things that can harm them. They need to be able to come to you to get that much- needed support when things get rough for them.

You, the parent, are the provider of what your child needs. There's a distinct difference between what is needed and what is wanted; they need:

FOOD	WATER	CLOTHING
HOME	LOVE	SUPPORT
EDUCATION	HEALTHCARE	SAFETY
TRUST	ENCOURAGEMENT	GUIDANCE
STRUCTURE	AFFECTION	REASSURANCE
LIMITATIONS	TRUTH	GOD

Give them the things they "want" for Christmas, birthdays, special occasions or to reward an accomplishment. But give them what they "need" on a daily basis.

We live in a materialistic society and that is often how we try to define our success to others. We don't find satisfaction unless we can outdo our next-door neighbors. (Even if it means we have to do without something we "need" so that we can get something that we "want.") And we're passing that on to our children.

No matter what their financial situation is, people will spend money on clothes, jewelry, alcohol, cigarettes or drugs instead of buying groceries. And we ask ourselves why our children act the way they do? It's because we are teaching them to act this way. Never tell your child to, "Do as I say, not as I do." If you find yourself saying those words, then what you're doing is more than likely an unacceptable behavior. There's a right way and a wrong way to do everything.

The majority of the African-American population has never been taught what to do with their money. The majority of our money is spent trying to make ends meet. Living from paycheck to paycheck is a constant struggle. And the struggle has gone on from one generation to another. So if it's your decision to become a single-parent, then do your child and yourself a favor preparing yourself by:

- RETURNING TO SCHOOL

- TAKING A CLASS ON FINANCES

- SAVING SOME MONEY

- LEARNING A NEW SKILL

- LEARNING A DIFFEENT LANGUAGE

- GETTING A JOB (OR A BETTER JOB)

- TAKING A CLASS ON EMPOWERMENT

- STARTING A BUSINESS

- GOING TO CHURCH OR READING YOUR BIBLE

- IMPROVING YOUR HEALTH

- GETTING DEPENDABLE TRANSPORTATION

- TAKING A PARENTING CLASS

- HAVING ADEQUATE SPACE IN YOUR HOME FOR YOU AND YOUR CHILD

You're reading this and thinking to yourself, no one does this. But do you know what? Some people sit down and plan out every aspect of their lives, and they call them goals. (Things they want to accomplish or do before they reach a particular age or stage of their life.)

Chart For Goals

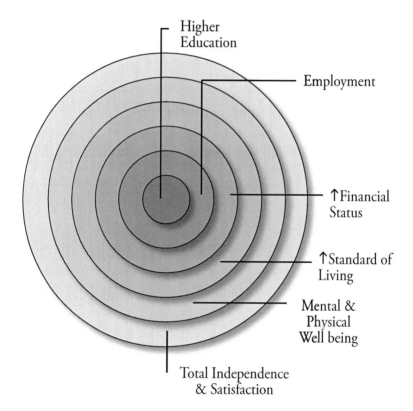

Higher Education

Employment

↑ Financial Status

↑ Standard of Living

Mental & Physical Well being

Total Independence & Satisfaction

When you set goals for yourself, other rewards begin to fall into place. You'll experience a sense of pride, confidence, self-awareness, a sense of accomplishment, increased communication skills, interaction with different people, self-respect, and respect, from others, personal growth, and an increased desire to learn and achieve more. You'll not only have what you need, you'll be able to get what you want. These are things that need to be passed on to your children, so they can pass them on to their children and their children's children.

You can be a very effective single-mother and raise a healthy child. However, remember the importance of the fact that EVERYTHING you do will be observed by your child. Everything! Therefore, prepare yourself well so that you are the best role model possible for your son or daughter. If you didn't learn how to become a great parent by observing your own parents, then it is so very important to follow the guidelines from this chapter so that you can begin to raise a healthy child that will undoubtedly turn into a healthy adult. Let it begin with you.

ABOUT THE AUTHOR

ANN E. WILLIAMSON

Ann E. Williamson is a minister, an inspirational speaker, professional coach and educator. In the year of 2005, she founded and is the Executive Director of a nonprofit organization called the Butterfly House, Inc. dedicated to serving women re-entering and reintegrating into society

Dr. Williamson is the owner and principal coach of Williamson Comprehensive Group. WCG specializes in coaching women who are executives, small business owners, and multi-faceted entrepreneurs.

Ann's educational background includes being a Graduate of Coach University. She has a Ph.D. in Holistic Counseling Ministry and. in Educational Administration. She also holds a M.Ed. in Instructional Leadership , a M.Ed. in Language Arts, and an A.B. Elementary Education.

She has trained coaches for Coach University's and Comprehensive Coaching U Professional Coach Training Programs. She is currently training Coaches through the Phoenix Coaching Institute, another entity she has founded. Dr. Ann taught for over twenty years in the Chicago Public Schools. Now she is teaching reading in the Coolidge Unified School District. Ann has led various leadership positions American Business Women Association. She is also on the advisory board of PWN.

Lastly, Dr. Williamson is the author of *Dr. Ann's 52 Prescriptions to Living Well by the Law* as well as the poetry book *Shedding*.

Contact:
Dr. Ann Williamson
(480) 892-7756
dranelwi@aol.com
www.annewilliamson.com
www.protrain.net

TEN

OVERCOMING THE BLAME GAME

By Dr. Ann E. Williamson

Take a look at your natural river. What are you?
Stop playing games with yourself. Where's your river going?
Are you riding with it? Or are you rowing against it?
Don't you see that there is no effort if you're riding with your river?"
—Frederick (Carl) Frieseke

As a child growing up, I can recall Santa always giving me wonderful presents. These presents would include clothing, dolls, oil painting kits, chemistry sets and games. Of course, not all of these things came at one time or every time. But it was guaranteed that I would get a game nearly every year. At such a young age, did I really know the importance of game playing? Or was I into the thrill of winning and having the competitive edge; or being in the game just for the fun of it? I learned at a very young age that playing games was an integral part of my life/being. I loved to play the board games or a game of checkers with my mother. At that time of my life, the television was being inundated with all kinds of game shows. I was hooked on Password and Concentration. I loved looking for new and interesting games to play with friends and family.

Dear Reader: Let's stop for a moment to list the kinds of games you played as a child and list the ones that have carried over into adulthood:

_____

_____

_____

_____

_____

What I didn't know then, is that life is a game such as the board games of Monopoly or Life. Not only is real life a game, but we also engage in a multitude of games throughout our daily lives. One particular book was written on this very subject, *Games People Play* (Berne). There is a game that I find very intriguing; it is the Blame Game. This is a game that has been around since Adam and Eve. You do remember the story of how the serpent persuaded Eve to take the apple from the tree of knowledge and eat it. She knew that she was not supposed to do so. She made the choice of picking and eating an apple rather than going for a long walk or meditating. Therefore, when she was asked about doing this ghastly deed, she said, "The devil made me do it." This is the first written account of when the Blame Game got started. It is still going on today.

Dear Reader: What does the Blame Game mean to you?

_____

_____

_____

_____

_____

We all have been there and played the game. Read the newspaper or listen to the news on any given day and you will see that this is one of the most popular games in the world. Playing this game is not delegated to one particular group of people. It is an equal opportunity game. Dr. Wayne Dyer has been quoted as saying, "All blame is a waste of time. No matter how much fault you find with another, and regardless of how much you blame him, it will not change you. The only thing blame does is to keep the focus off you when you are looking for external reasons to explain your unhappiness or frustration. You may succeed in making another feel guilty about something by blaming him, but you won't succeed in changing whatever it is about you that is making you unhappy."

I decided to interview a few of my friends in the inner circle to see what their responses were in regard to playing the Blame Game. The first question that I asked them was, what is the Blame Game? Their answers included the following:

Al: "The Blame Game is when you blame others for all your problems and do not take responsibility for your participation or your responses."

Mario added: "It is clever and subtle; it is a way to avoid responsibility for an undesired circumstance."

Michelle: "Being a victim of circumstances and not willing to be accountable or to deal with results responsibly."

Tim: "If I blame you, then "it" is not my fault, but yours. This keeps me in the victim position, leaving me helpless or hurt or angry or a combination of similar emotions. I get to continue my old story and take little or no action. Remember, I am the victim and cannot help myself. Hmm, I need someone to care of me. I am not taking responsibility for myself...any way.... no how!"

Dear Reader: Let's stop for a moment to write what your thoughts are about what my friends (above) said about the Blame Game.

_____

_____

_____

_____

_____

I get it now. It is a game without a board! The second leg of my quest to find answers led me to the next question. I asked my colleagues what the rules were, as they perceived them to be? These rules may be written or unstated, and run the gamut. Their answers included these responses:

- "Anything goes: Proclaim their guilt loudly to anyone who will listen."

- "There are no rules."

- "Only one rule: It's not my fault. Nothing ever..."

- "Throw your rock and hide your hand. Make yourself a victim."

- "The rules are pretty one sided (your own) because very rarely do we tell others that we are blaming them for something."

- "Simply put, find someone who will play! You can smell them, can't you? Most likely it will be someone who is coming from a place of fear. If you cannot find someone to play with, don't worry!!! Blame, rationalizations and resentments can be created quite efficiently within the space of just one person's mind! In fact, that seems to be a method of choice."

- "The only rule is that of the ego trying to protect itself from having to look at its own shadow. The ego will do anything to escape having to admit that it is short of perfect, and having someone else to blame."

Dear Reader: Let's stop for a moment to write the rules by which you have played:

_____

_____

_____

_____

_____

Dear Reader: Please take the time to write the players in your game of blame. Tell why you chose them to play with you.

_____

_____

_____

_____

_____

The third question that I asked my friends was as to whether they personally have played the Blame Game and what the outcome was . They replied by saying:

- "People hearing the outright guilt assessment may engage in "ain't it awful" conversations.

- "Blaming others and being a victim. No wins."

- "I try never to play the Blame Game, but probably have in relationships that I no longer want to be in. It's always easier to not take the responsibility for actions in a relationship. The relationships would end and then you felt no guilt, because you made it the others fault. Probably the outcome is that I am still alone. Not a fun outcome, huh?"

- "Years ago…and all I got was the universe having me do it all over again until it was done right."

- "I think we have all played the Blame Game. The Blame Game is pretty lonely. If you don't forgive and move on, you carry a lot of baggage that is best to let go of. If you continue to carry that baggage, you slow down - it's a heavy load to carry. Inevitably, I am left with a feeling of low self-esteem, with a dash of embarrassment, flavored with shame. That is, once I am willing to claim my part in the game!"

- "I've played the game by not facing my own role in creating a tense and unworkable situation, choosing instead to blame others. The outcome was that the truth was found out, and I did have to ultimately face my personal responsibility for my part in. The good news is that I took an important personal growth step by doing so."

Dear Reader: Please answer the following question: Have you played the Blame Game, and are you still playing it?

_____

_____

_____

_____

_____

The last question was why play the game in the first place? Their answers included these:

- "Depends on the kind of person. It's seen all the time with passive aggressive and those who don't want to take responsibility for their own behaviors."

- "To avoid responsibility for my own life, perceived failure, undesired circumstance."

- "Fear, lack of self esteem, just do not care."

- "The game is usually played when we are not speaking up for ourselves and letting others know what we are thinking and feeling. If you don't take responsibility for your own happiness, no one else can."

- "Who says it starts as a choice? Perhaps it started as an instinctual means of survival. Maybe, I am afraid my Daddy will not love me if he knows that I am the one who broke the lawnmower. I better put the blame on my little brother, in case Daddy finds out; he'll still love me - maybe not my little Brother."

- "As I said above, we play the game because our egos, with which we identify, fear "losing face." Rather than face our faults and limitations, we do anything to avoid them, and cast the blame on someone else."

Dear Reader: If you have played and are still playing the Blame Game, why did you play in the first place?

_____

_____

_____

_____

_____

To play the Blame Game, it all goes back to one of our beliefs in knowing and accepting who we really are. Who we are, really aligns with that divine energy that flows through our bodies. This who is at the center of our very being. If one does not know this, then a person will begin to feel inadequate, worthless, and not enough. Then one begins to play the Blame Game and becomes very proficient at it.

It was becoming very clear to me why this game has lasted as long as it has in our culture (as well as throughout the world). Before I stopped this quest, I asked the inner- circle for any final words to share with me about the Blame Game.

These were their final words:

- "I passed along time ago on game playing. I think it's for the poor little victim or the manipulator. I am neither. I also see it for those who will step on anyone or blame anyone to get higher up the ladder."

- "First of all, I'm not a person who blames others - I take my own "hits" and own up to my mistakes, once I know I've made them. I think people who blame others, when blame is not due to them, are cowards. Personally, I'd rather not have anything to do with these cowards."

• "Be responsible for your own behaviors and see your partner accountable for his/hers."

• "If you find yourself blaming others for every possible problem that exists in your workplace, then you may be in the burnout loop of blaming others to make up for and hide your lack of enthusiasm."

• "It's pretty popular in today's American culture; [it's] entertaining; also a great diversion from effecting the desired outcome; but mean, nasty, and detrimental to most everyone who plays it!"

• "At some point, every reasoning person, who knows he or she exists each day, by the grace of God alone, has to face the truth of who they really are. You'll live by the consequences, either way."

• "When I was foolish enough to "play" the Blame Game, I think it left me (as Iyanla Vanzant might say), "SOS = Stuck on Stupid.""

• "Yes, it's a worthless game designed to disempower ourselves and others when we play it."

• "When you start blaming others, its time to look inside to ask yourself why you have allowed them to make you feel 'less than'."

• "It takes willingness and courage to look at one's self in an honest way. Until this is done, it is easy to keep blaming. Pain also happens to be a great motivator that dares us to look within and make the change to better our lives and our world."

• "I think it's a built-in part of our lives, as long as we identify with our personal egos or "small self." As we progress on the spiritual path, we learn that we are not our egos, but rather we are spiritual beings having a human experience. Then we can more easily laugh at ourselves and not take ourselves so seriously, and rather than seeking to protect our egos, we seek opportunities to face our weaknesses and learn to do better."

Dear Reader: What are your thoughts about the Blame Game now?

_____

_____

_____

_____

I can laugh at myself as I come to the end of this quest. For if I continue to reflect upon days of yesteryear, I can say honestly that I, too, have joined in the playing of the Blame Game. I can remember telling others that something didn't happen in my life because I was of African decent, my gender was female, or didn't have money like "other" people. Yes, I blamed others and myself.

Yes, this is playing the victim, the perfect player of the game. Did I feel any better because I was blaming another group of people? Of course not!

The Toolkit for Overcoming the Blame Game:

Tool #1: **Surrender.** Yes, surrender to your greater power. In this way, you can let God handle all of the details. This can be accomplished with a prayer. Let go and let God!

Dear Reader: Here is an example of a prayer you can say and model your own prayer after.

Divine God dwelling within me, through and around me, I speak these words. I open my body, mind and soul to you right here and right now. As I release the need or desire to blame others for things that have occurred or is occurring in my life that is not to my liking, I let the presence of God enter into these places. I accept the love, peace, joy, and wisdom to turn the events around to create within me a new heart and a new life. I take responsibility for all things that appear in my life. I know that my silent but very powerful partner, God, is working out all the details to make all things right. All this is so and I give thanks to God in knowing that it is so. Amen

Tool #2: **Affirmations.** Saying positive statements of truth when I find myself going down that road to play the Blame Game. Affirmations can help me stay focused on taking responsibility for my actions. It also helps me to know that I do have choices in life. *I have the strength to endure any obstacle by taking full responsibility for it.*

Dear Reader: Please take the time to write an affirmation. Remember to write in the present time and use positive words.

_____

_____

_____

_____

_____

Tool #3: **Meditation.** By meditating, I mean to sit still and listen to the answers to your prayers. God does give answers through signs or gentle nudgings within your being. Choose the perfect space to center yourself in the calmness of God. Let yourself be open for the signs to appear to you.

Exercise:

Dear Reader: Please take the time to practice this example of a meditation. (Play some soft music in the background and have a candle burning.) Go to a quiet place.

Begin your meditation with stillness and tranquility. Close your eyes and take a deep breath. Relax your body and mind. Take a few deep breaths, and each time you exhale, feel your body relax into a serene state. Let go of your worries, concerns and cares. Feel only the presence of God within, through, and around you. As you settle into this place where love and peace are, place your right hand over the area of your heart. Keeping your right hand in this position, bring the left hand to your right wrist and locate your pulse. In this position, relax quietly, feeling both your heartbeat and pulse beat for a minute or two until you feel thoroughly concentrated on these inner workings of your body. Visualize in your mind that God is there beside you. Visualize that all cares and worries are given to God. That all people, places and things no longer exist in your life that was part of the Blame Game.

Tool #4: **Inspirational Reading and Tapes.** Keep them handy to fortify your faith. To help get past the urge to play the Blame Game.

Tool #5: **Forgive.** Surely, forgiveness is one of the hardest requests to fulfill for most people. Next to surrendering, it is a difficult thing to do. Forgiveness is an act of love. Forgiveness allows one to grow into one's brilliance of being the victor and not the victim. As a result, one may be disqualified from playing the Blame Game.

Dear Reader: Please take the time to write a list of those people that need to be forgiven, including your self.

1. _____

2. _____

3. _____

4. _____

Playing the Blame Game can be an addicting habit that can be reversed. Dr. 0. Battista said, "Placing the blame is a bad habit, but taking the blame is a sure builder of character." I still enjoy playing certain games, whether they are Wheel of Fortune on television, or Taboo out of the box. However, I have decided never to play the old Blame Game again. May you, the reader, build character by being accountable for any errors or misgivings that you may have caused. It is difficult to admit guilt or wrongdoings, but have the confidence that you can do it!

Dear Reader: What are your afterthoughts about not playing the Blame Game, and where do you go from here?

_____

_____

_____

_____

ABOUT THE AUTHOR

KAREN R. FREEMAN-MOORE

Karen R. Freeman, President and Founder of The E.T.N. Group, believes wholeheartedly in the power of self-discovery and action planning. Her strong background in human services, human resources and training provides her with an excellent foundation to assist her clients with their stated goals.

The E.T.N. Group is a personal and professional development company designed to "unlock" the client's potential for further growth and fulfillment.

The E.T.N. Group workshops are designed to provide a higher level of awareness-whether for a business professional seeking better customer relation skills, a mother-daughter who want to enhance their communication, or a child who has questions about those different from his/her.

Karen Freeman and her daughter, Victoria, live in Charlotte, North Carolina.

Contact:
The E.T.N. Group
P.O. Box 480635
Charlotte, NC 28269
(704) 921-3052
ETNgroup@bellsouth.net
www.protrain.net

ELEVEN

SAYING GOODBYE: DEALING WITH GRIEF

By Karen Freeman-Moore

SWEET PEACE
Brother, the sweet peace of knowing your pain is no more, comforts me.
Daddy, the sweet peace in your face
as you raised it to us one last time, reassures me.
Mama, the sweet peace that comes from
witnessing your courage when they left us; soothes me.
For as I lift mine eyes onto the heavens from which cometh God's help,
Sweet peace makes it all bearable.

My Personal Reflection

Early in 2003, no one could have told me that soon we would lose two precious members of our family. Although my brother had lived with Sarcoidosis for over seven years, in and out of the hospital with lung-related ailments, we almost never thought, "This is it." But, after a hard-fought battle, the day finally came when, "this was it" and he did not return home. Gregory was forty-three years old.

My father's death came as a complete shock. Yes, he had open-heart surgery several years before. Yes, he had been a long-time smoker. Yes, he had worked for over thirty years at Reagan National Airport, driving 70 miles each way. And yes, he had also been a successful small business owner all of my life. But no one expected him to have a heart attack one week after burying his middle child. He survived his second open-heart surgery after a rocky period. He was released from the hospital mid-September and then released by his doctor just two days before his heart failed for the last time. Maybe he just didn't want my brother to be lonely in heaven.

Down here on Earth, my family mourned. We grieved. We grieve still.

When the opportunity came for me to participate in the co-authoring of this book, I was speaking with a friend about the subject I had chosen. His comment was, "That's odd, because I didn't think that you had ever grieved." His words hit me hard, because I had never really thought about how long or how demonstrative a person's grief had to be in order for others to feel that you're doing "it" right. I believe grief has many faces.

So, how do we do it? Is there really a right way to grieve? No, of course there isn't. During our lives we learn how to love and how to protect the people we love from hurt and harm. The miracle of life is often at the heart of many movies and television shows. We celebrate living! Then somewhere along the way, we learn that death and letting go is also a part of life. At a young age, we learn that friendships sometimes end and we have to let go. We learn that romantic relationships can end and how much that can hurt, but we have to let go. Realistically, we know that we may never see that person again. However, for the most part, people will move past those rough times and move on with their lives. Yet, those early experiences of loss and hurt do not prepare us for the "letting go" we face when a loved one dies. Death and grief hit us at the core of our being.

I honestly do not believe that we ever stop grieving entirely. But, rather, we learn to "deal". We may never stop longing for our loved one's presence. The missed birthdays, holidays, weddings and births may all be experienced with unshed tears as we reflect on their absence from our special celebrations. I miss my brother and father every day. The smallest thing may happen which reminds me of them. For example, each time that I hear Luther Vandross' song, "Dance With My Father", my heart quickens for a moment as I think about my own father. When I see my niece and nephew arguing one moment and hugging the next, I clearly see my brother and me in those two. However, I do believe that in order to achieve peace in our lives, we must grow in understanding and acceptance of our loved one's death. It takes time.

I have no magic cures. But, what I can do is put into words emotions that you may be feeling, offer you a path to deal with your loss, and processes that may ease your heart and ultimately, lift your spirit.

At the beginning of each pathway below are the inner-thoughts of someone who's grieving. After reading their message, close your eyes and let their words, their passage from hurt to renewal, sit in your spirit for a moment. Then, when you are ready, begin your own journey by listening to heart and mind as you start on:

A Pathway From Grief to P.E.A.C.E.

Proverbs 3 (NIV)

(5) Trust in the Lord with all your heart and lean not on your own understanding; (6) and in all your ways acknowledge him, and he will direct your path.

(13) Blessed is the man who finds wisdom, the man who gains understanding, (14) for she is more profitable than silver and yields better returns than gold. (18) She is the tree of life to those who embrace her and those who lay hold of her will be blessed.

(24) When you lie down, you will not be afraid; when you lie down, your sleep will be sweet. (26) For the Lord will be your confidence...

Pathway I - From Painful and Powerless to Patience and Purposeful:

I want to run from the pain in my heart and the powerlessness in my spirit! Yet, I beg my heart and spirit to be patient while I heal. As time passes, my burden lifts from within and my spirit rejoices with renewed strength and purpose. I can finally breathe.

Step I

Painful and Powerless – As I sit quietly with my grief, during my darkest hour, I feel:

_____

_____

_____

_____

_____

_____

Patience and Purposeful – I recognize that I need time to heal. I will allow myself that time and work toward rediscovering my purpose by:

_____

_____

_____

_____

_____

_____

Pathway II - From Engulfed and Enraged to Encouraged and Engaged

Oh, anger you engulf my soul as I try to make sense of this senseless death! You WILL NOT consume me! Tears flow from the loss of my unborn son. "My child?" God calls out. He grabs my attention and engages me in conversation. "Be encouraged for I am with you always," He says. After a while, my anger slowly subsides.

Step II

Engulfed and Enraged – Do I have the "right" to be consumed with this anger? My friends and family do not seem to understand. If I am honest with myself, I am most angry because:

_____

_____

_____

_____

_____

_____

Encouraged and Engaged – I understand that long-term feelings of anger may cause me emotional and physical harm. I will make all efforts to accept encouragement from people who love me. I will take steps to become more engaged in my life. I will begin by:

_____

_____

_____

_____

_____

_____

Pathway III - From Abandoned and Anguished to Acceptance and Appreciation

"He's dying!" she thought. "He's abandoning me. After forty-seven years of marriage, how can I go on living? I can't do anything without him!" His wife looks upon his face and he whispers his love for her. Then his eyes plead for her to accept God's plan. Through a stream of tears, she releases him to the angels and tenderly appreciates all that he was.

Step III

Abandoned and Anguished – Being alone can be very frightening. My biggest fear(s) about being by myself is/are:

_____

_____

_____

_____

_____

_____

Acceptance and Appreciation – I have listened to my inner thoughts and my fear of abandonment. I am slowly coming to terms with my loved one's death. These are the things that make me smile when I think about him/her and I will always appreciate and treasure:

_____

_____

_____

_____

_____

_____

Pathway IV - From Chaos and Confusion to Coping and Clarity

So much to do! So much to do! Well-meaning people with words of condolences stop by every few minutes. "How can I help?" they ask. " I DON'T KNOW!" I want to scream! "My daughter has been lost to the violent streets!" Chaos and confusion cloud my mind. When will I begin to cope with all of this? "Soon," say family. "Soon," say friends. "SOON," says my Father with finality. I pray. Yes, clarity will come soon.

Step IV

Chaos and Confusion – Making decisions when a loved one dies can be stressful. Right now, I am overwhelmed because:

_____

_____

_____

_____

_____

_____

Coping and Clarity – I know there is no shame in asking for help. I will not be afraid to seek guidance. These are the people I trust and the agencies that I can contact to help me cope with my loss:

_____

_____

_____

_____

_____

_____

Pathway V - From Elusive and Encumbered to Embracing and Enlightened

For a long while, happiness eludes my grasp. I am encumbered by my fear and guilt of moving on without you. I am learning to embrace God's wisdom and lean on Him for enlightenment and understanding. Each day I take another step towards sweet peace.

Step V

Elusive and Encumbered – Right now, happiness may seem far away. The feelings that most weigh down on me are:

_____

_____

_____

_____

_____

_____

Embracing and Enlightened – God's message is clear that I must trust Him with my hurt in order to heal my spirit. I will do this by:

_____

_____

_____

_____

_____

_____

A Prayer For Your Journey to P.E.A.C.E

My God, today I pray that your child (this reader) finds sweet peace in the comfort of your Word. Guide them to seek counsel from those who know your healing power. Let them open their hearts and minds in order to mend from the inside, out. My Father, embrace them and rock them until the pain has eased. May they understand and believe that you are with them ALWAYS! Amen.

With my brother and father's death, it helped me to know that they both were ready. My brother, with the help of angels, released himself from the constraints of a three-day coma. As he raised his hand to heaven and tears slipped through his closed eyes, his soul ascended in peace. My father left us a message the day before he died. It simply said, "Going home." His face looked more at rest than I had seen it look in a very long time.

So, when my friend said that he didn't think I had grieved, he simply didn't understand the sweet peace that overshadowed my grief. Although sometimes I still mourn their death, I feel that they are always close by. I often ask for their protection as I travel or to watch over my mother and daughter. I also give honor to them everyday. I have my father's 1952 prom picture as my computer screen saver! A "Gregory" angel figurine sits on my kitchen window and I thank God for having had my brother's presence in my life.

I encourage you to find a special way to acknowledge and honor your loved one's life. It may be the catalyst that begins your **Pathway to Sweet P.E.A.C.E**

May God bless you, always.

Notes:

ABOUT THE AUTHOR

Myrtle Looby

Myrtle Looby is the President and Primary Consultant of LEAP Training Consultants, based in Antigua and Barbuda. Having enjoyed a successful career as a trained educator of English and Communication Skills, she now makes keynote presentations, and designs and conducts outstanding workshops and training seminars throughout the Caribbean. Some of her most sought after workshops are on Customer Care, Communication Skills, Leadership, Effective Supervision, Team Building and Women's Issues.

Myrtle's background and expertise have contributed to the passion and dynamism that she brings to all aspects of her life, including community service. She is a founding member of the Professional Organization of Women in Antigua/Barbuda (P.O.W.A.), a member of the Advisory Committee of the Directorate of Gender Affairs in Antigua and Barbuda and a member of the Antigua Lions Club. As a Lion, she has held the position of Zone Chairperson, Region Chairperson, and District Trainer for District 60B. She is also an active member of her church community where she uses her expertise to conduct seminars with the Young Adults Group. Internationally, she serves on the Board of Advisors of The Professional Woman Network and is a member of the Professional Woman Speakers Bureau.

In fulfilling one of her lifelong dreams she has co-authored the recently published best-sellers, *Becoming the Professional Woman*, and *The Young Woman's Guide to Personal Success*. She is currently working on her sixth publication.

Myrtle holds a Bachelor of Arts in English and History, a Diploma in Education, a Certificate in Guidance Counseling and a Diploma in Gender and Development Studies.

Contact:
LEAP Training Consultants
P.O. Box W704 Woods Centre
St. John's, Antigua
(268) 460-5504
guidance@candw.ag
www.prowomen.net

TWELVE

SPEAK UP! COMMUNICATING WITH POWER AND AUTHORITY

By Myrtle Looby

"Our worst fear is not that we are inadequate; our deepest fear is that we are powerful beyond measure. It is our light, not our darkness that most frightens us. We ask ourselves, 'Who am I to be so brilliant, gorgeous, talented and fabulous?' Actually, who are we not to be? You are a child of God: Your playing small doesn't serve the world. There is nothing enlightening about shrinking so that other people won't feel insecure around you." — Marianne Williamson

Marianne Williamson could well have been refering to us, African-American women, who are confident in many ways, but often do not demonstrate power and authority when we communicate! We may be "brilliant, gorgeous, talented....fabulous," and "powerful beyond measure," yet we often complain that we experience frustration and disappointment by being unacknowledged, disrespected, unappreciated, ignored, overlooked, or not taken seriously. This can happen at work, in social groups, religious or civic organizations, and even in academia. Why, then is this so? Is it that we are guilty of "shrinking", or not using our personal power so that others would feel more secure around us? Or is it out of ignorance – not knowing how to speak with confidence?

Williamson continues, "*We were born to make manifest the glory of God within us. It is not just in some of us, it is in everyone. And as we let our own light shine, we unconsciously give other people permission to do the same. As we are liberated from our own fear, our presence automatically liberates others.*"

Do we let "our own light shine" by the way we communicate? Does fear of speaking up imprison us? Let's find out.

If you are asked whether you speak with power and authority, the answer would be a resounding "Yes." In fact, when we look at the image of the African-American woman perpetuated by some popular sitcoms, we are portrayed as fast talking, hip shaking, finger pointing, no-nonsense women who know how to use all we've got to get our message across. The truth is that while we are able to speak more freely and confidently in some situations, in others, we give our power away! We are usually more confident at home, or in all-female informal groups, but at work or in mixed groups, our power and confidence often seem to dissipate.

Women of color are in a double or triple bind because of subtle or overt forms of bias based on gender, ethnicity and social class steroetypes. Our authority and credibility are often questioned, but before we jump to conclusions as the "victim" and assign blame, we need to examine whether our communication styles are sabotaging our own success.

Chances are that we communicate in the language of powerlessness, both verbally and non-verbally, and therefore do not demonstrate the authority we possess and gain the respect we deserve.

It is often said that language is power, but in reality, real power comes not from language itself, but from our ability to use language, verbal and non-verbal, to get our message across and achieve the desired intention. Proficiency in using the language of power brings rewarding results and is central to our personal and professional survival.

Successful women depend on their ability to communicate using language as a bag of tools. Knowing which tool should be used, how, when and where, makes for success on and off the job. To a friend of mine, language is like her make-up kit. How and when she uses each item or combination of items is determined by the occasion and impression she wishes to create with others. Similarly, how creatively we make use of the keys on our computer keyboard and the icons on our desktop, will determine how much power we achieve in our presentations!

Let us now review some of the areas that can undermine our power and authority when we communicate. You can take a personal inventory, and if you are in doubt you may ask a friend to assist you.

• When you enter a room, is your stride even? When you stand to speak, is your body erect, with head held high, shoulders relaxed, chin up and eyes making contact with your listeners?

- Is your handshake firm and do you address others by their names?

- Are your clothes well tailored and co-ordinated, and is the cut, color and style suited to your body size and shape? Are they appropriate for the occasion?

- Do your make-up and hairstyle compliment your beauty or mask it?

- How about your oral and general hygiene habits? Are they exemplary?

- Do you speak with confidence so that others will take notice?

- Is your speech of a moderate pace that facilitates listening?

- How about your pitch and tone? Are they strident or rambunctious, inaudible or muffled? Or are they well modulated and "easy on the ears?"

- Can you utilize silence as a powerful tool to maintain control of a situation?

- Does your speech style match your intention (i.e. Do you frame your sentences as questions when you mean to make statements?)

- In a conversation, do you cut others off before they complete their comment?

- Do you often use verbal hedges like "in my opinion" to soften the impact of a statement, as though not wanting to offend?

- Are you often apologizing when making a point, for example, by tagging, "I may be wrong, but…"?

- Do you use fillers as "um," "er" or "you know what I mean"?

- Do you repeat phrases or sentences as "in terms of" or "you see what I'm saying"?

- Do you feel more comfortable with slang or colloquialisms instead of the more widely accepted forms of English?

- Are your words well-enunciated, especially at the last syllables?

- Have you been reading widely and can you converse resonably well on current events?

- Is your vocabulary wide and varied and do your words convey the precise meaning?

- Do your verbs agree with their subject or do you use double negatives?

Your responses may reveal what many women are guilty of. They are SABOTAGING THEIR OWN SUCCESS! However, like with Donna Belle below, help is on the way.

Donna Belle, CEO

Donna Belle, the new CEO of a large Human Resource organization, had heard through the grapevine that she was being considered for a promotion because of her length of service and vast experience in the personnel department. Although she possessed the required qualifications, her one drawback was that her contributions at meetings were weak and did not reflect authority. In fact, among her other shortcomings was that her comments were often in the form of questions rather than bold assertive statements. The CEO wondered whether she would have been able to hold her own around the negotiation table with clients and aggressive trade union representatives.

But Donna Belle was determined to move up the ladder, so before her interviews, she assessed her communication style and identified areas that needed improvement. She sought out mentors whose communication styles she admired and wished to emulate, and contacted them for their guidance. She also purchased videotapes of keynote speakers and viewed television interviews with reputable hosts. She used a tape recorder to listen to her own voice and made adjustments. She utilized her "girls network" as her Personal Board of Directors to evaluate her progress and provide feedback.

It was no surprise that at the final interview, she surpassed all the other candidates and landed the promotion. Now, she has developed her own personal style and communicates with greater confidence. She is still working on the challenge of communicating more effectively by registering for personal development courses and seminars, and she has joined a leadership development organization where her skills can be nurtured.

Let us look at some strategies that successful women utilize to communicate with more power and confidence, and some that raise red flags.

Develop a Winning and Positive Attitude

Like with Donna Belle, a positive attitude determines our altitude. Women who speak with power and authority set goals for personal development and strive to accomplish them. If we look at successful African-American women, we would realize that they have also liberated themselves from the limiting beliefs dictated by gender, social class or color, that threaten to undermine their self esteem and self-confidence.

Take Note of Your Resources, Strengths and Areas for Improvement

If we choose to maximise our potential for success and break through any barriers, we must also take note of the resources to leverage our strengths and improve in our weak areas. Topping the list of our self-affirming resources are: our rich heritage and cultural background, our unique and creative communication styles, our mentors and role models, and our informal network of sisterfriends. Let them work for us. In addition, we are intelligent, competent, resourceful and creative, and since we are made in God's image, we are well made. We choose not to allow other people's opinions of us to define who we are.

Build Assertiveness

We build assertiveness by being prepared, through continuous personal and professional development and practice. We become knowledgable about issues and put our brain in action before we begin to speak. We are attentive listeners and learn from others. We accept responsibility and are not afraid to make mistakes, as these are learning experiences. When we are wrong, we gracefully accept blame and apologize, but when we are not, we don't. We indicate how we would make amends, solve the problem or prevent a reoccurence, but we do not berate ourselves or grovel. This retards progress, and is demeaning and unbecoming of an empowered woman.

Communicate Assertively

Maralyn Stewart Miller, in "*Becoming the Professional Woman*", states that to gain clarity, we utilize three types of communication: Assertive, Aggressive and Non-Assertive or Passive. However, the preferred type for business and positive relationships is **Assertive Communication,** which is "clear, direct, specific and timely." It allows us to stand up for ourselves and claim our right to speak without infringing the rights of others.

Dianne M. Daniels, Image and Color Consultant, advises women to communicate assertively by paying attention to the Visual, Vocal and Verbal, a combination which she refers to as the Total Image Concept. Psychologist Albert Mehrabian claims that 55% of our communication is non-verbal, our tone is responsible for 38% and our words a mere 7%.

The visual is what others see when we present ourselves to them, and in a few seconds, they can determine whether we are to be taken seriously or not. It includes our body language, poise and posture, physical features, facial expression, skin tone, hair, nails and make-up, general hygiene, the cut, color and fit of our clothes, and accessories.

If we are uncomfortable with our bodies, it would impact negatively on our self-confidence and diminish our power to communicate effectively. Beyond our genes, we can improve our body image by shedding excess weight and wearing appropriate clothing. The cut and color of our clothing should enhance our figure and complexion, and our make-up and accessories should complement our beauty.

The vocal refers to the sound of our voice, the volume, tone, pitch and rate of speech.

It is our speech, more than the written word, that we use to communicate our ideas, opinions and values. Our language also reflects how we think about ourselves, whether we are leaders or followers, or whether or not we possess self-confidence.

Vocal style can also be a boon or hindrance to communication. Apart from the words, a speaker's tone, volume, pitch and speed convey ideas and feelings and open a window to her physical and emotional state.

Here is a fun exercise for you. It is a quote by Ellen Johnson-Sirleaf, President of Liberia. You can read it aloud to someone, paying attention to your vocal style.

"As African women, we've had to compete more than women in the developed societies. But this has compelled us to be more aggressive in trying to reach the highest levels. We're knocking at the door, and there is a little crack in it. If I win, many other women will push on it. And then it's going to open."

- Did you vary the volume of your voice for emphasis and to maintain the listener's interest?

- I am sure you also varied the tone between high and low, but not too high as to be strident or too low to be monotonous. Either extreme would make you lose your ability to influence the listener.

- Was your pronounciation clear and crisp, especially with those "th" words, and endings like in "compelled," "highest," and "knocking"? These seem to be minor details, but good pronunciation gives your communication elegance and polish and facilitates listening.

- Did you speak with a moderate speed so that the listener would understand you, or did he/she have to hang on to each word? Was your breathing even?

Where did you put more warmth or energy when reading? Most readers would put some passion in the latter part of the quotation, from "We're knocking at the door...." to show energy and enthusiasm. I am sure you did!

Now, re-read the passage and check to see whether this time, you read with greater impact. Remember, practice makes improvement!

The verbal includes our vocabulary, grammar and sentence style. Many of us believe that it is our listeners' duty to understand our way of speaking and not **our** duty to speak in a language that is more universally understood. Communication only becomes effective when the desired message is recieved. Ebonics, with its own gramatical structure and syntax, (like double negatives in "He ain't got no business going there.") may be accepted within the African-American community, but it has limited viability when we communicate with other groups. While versatility of communication styles would increase our credibility and give us more leaverage with wider audiences, proficiency in English is an asset in business communication.

In addition, a rich and varied vocbulary gives successful women the facility to communicate more effectively in a variety of situations. As our vocabulary increases, we no longer need the fillers as , "uhm," " er," or "you know what I'm saying?" and we are no longer embarrassed by the wrong choice of words.

I have always admired a colleague who consistently manages to convey the precise meaning, from her repertoire of action verbs, and vivid adjectives and adverbs. She is an avid reader and no doubt her passion for crossword puzzles has equipped her with the right words instead of less effective synonyms. A good dictionary and thesaurus always occupy a prominent place on her desk.

Hedging

Confident speakers avoid hedging, that is, hiding behind words that merely lenghten sentences, add no value to the communication, and diminish their self worth. Hedging also conveys indecision and lack of commitment. Instead, women of power use sentences that are more assertive.

Here are some examples.

Hedging:	*"In my opinion, the mecessary steps should be taken to avoid any delay."*
Assertive:	*"The necessary steps should be taken to avoid any delay."*
Hedging:	*"The way I see it, length of service must be considered when making recommendations for promotion."*
Assertive:	*"Length of service should be considered when we make recommendations for promotion."*
Hedging:	*"Don't get me wrong, but I do not appreciate your sexist jokes in the office."*
Assertive:	*"I do not appreciate your making sexist jokes in the office and I ask that you desist."*

The "I" Statements

If you have the tendency to begin your sentences with "I", check whether you are talking about yourself. Phyllis Mindell, in *How to Say it for Women,* identifies "the indicisive I" that characterizes the speech of many professional women. We draw attention to ourselves, even though we are not the subject of the sentence. Here are three examples of the

"I" statements that weaken our language: By revising the sentence to begin with the subject, our speech becomes more definite and precise.

Indecisive	Definite and Precise
"I think it is difficult for us to decide on a date today because I am not sure whether everyone knows about this meeting."	*"We will not be able to decide on a date today because everyone might not have been notified about this meeting."*
"I notice that whenever I arrive at work the air condition unit is off. Why is that?"	*"Why is the air condition unit off whenever I arrive at work?"*
"I cannot say that this is the way I prefer it but you can try it differently next time."	*"This is not the way I prefer to have it done, so you can try it differently next time."*

Tagging

Tagging is a speech pattern common to women. It is the practice of adding short questions to the end of sentences in an attempt to gain consensus. At best, the sentences can invite comments for discussion, but more often they convey uncertainty and weaken the power of our statements. For example:

"I usually purchase my supplies wholesale, you know what I'm saying?"
"Whenever it rains, the car park is flooded, see what I mean?"
"Please prepare this document for my meeting this afternoon, okay?"

When we remove the "tags", we speak with greater confidence and earn credibility and respect.

False Questions

Perhaps some of us see ourselves as undeserving of power and authority, despite our position or academic qualifications. We further weaken our position by raising our voice at the end of a sentence, as though we are asking a question, or after making a statement we shrug our shoulders and use other self-deprecating body language. For example, *"We would like you to make your presentation within the allotted time(?)."* It is possible that we do so to win friends and gain acceptance, or so as not to appear aggressive or bossy. However, when we can affirm our selves and feel comfortably empowered, we indicate a clear difference between our statements and questions. Continuous practice would bring positive results in this area.

Colloquialism

Another example of powerless communication is the use of colloquialisms, especially with younger women. For example, "this is so ..... not cool," "it's like....," "....you know" "what ever!" and non-words such as "thingy," "irregardless" and "conversate." Another blunder is using big words that sound impressive but are not, as some recently coined verbs that end in "ize."

Passive Voice

While effective communication utilizes both the active and passive voice, the former proves to be more clear, concise and direct, and the latter, weak, impersonal and sometimes cumbersome. For example,

(Passive) "Fish are caught in the lake whenever we go on vacation," instead of *(Active) "Whenever we go on vacation, we catch fish in the lake."*

However, if constructed properly, the passive voice can be a powerful tool to establish distance, soften comments and maintain control, especially in positions of authority, as in, *"Absence without permission will be regarded as abandonment of duty."* So think about what you want to say and how it can be communicated most effectively using language and tone. Then choose either the active or passive voice to convey your message.

Male/Female Communication Styles

Males and females use different communication styles, and it would be to our benefit to be aware of the differences and make them work for us. I have discussed some of them in *Becoming the Professional Woman*, but it is worth mentioning a few here.

Males speak boldly about their accomplishments while females, not wanting to "boast or brag," tend to diminish theirs or consider them the result of "luck." Men usually apologise for their weaknesses, women for their strengths. Be assertive. Blow your own horn and do not apologise for your success.

At meetings, males assert themselves by claiming their space! You do the same. Don't box yourself in. Establish control of more space. Be relaxed and use a few gestures, the correct posture, speech and appearance to exude self-confidence and personal power. Let them work for you!

Stereotyping

Communicating with power and authority also requires astute leadership skills. It is said that a balance of power and good interpersonal relations build rapport with our listeners without our being pushy and obnoxious. However, the stereotypical qualities ascribed to women, and women of color, give rise to certain expectations that may prove challenging. Though we are complimented for being confident, powerful and competent, even as professional women, we are expected to be nurturing, helpful, maternal and sociable. When others' expectations of us are not met, we are accused of being un-feminine, or labeled with the B word.

Some persons may feel offended by your assertiveness, out of ignorance. When this occurs, don't take it personally. It's not about you. It is important, though, that we monitor others' perceptions of us as we communicate. Our intention should be to demonstrate authority, tempered with warmth and empathy, without being threatening or overbearing to others.

Difficult Situations

Women of power know how to hande difficult situations. Sarcasm, expletives, crying or making deregotary comments may amuse or impress some but would devalue the speaker. Keep your cool and composure even when "your cup boileth over." If you can, say to yourself, "This is a test, this is only a test, and this, too, shall pass." It will! If possible, step out of the room for a while and return when you have regained control of your emotions. Remember: "A woman is like a tea leaf. When she gets in hot water, she just gets stronger." Strength begins on the inside!

Sisters, our survival depends on our ability to communicate effectively, individually and collectively. So stand up, stand out and speak up – with power and authority!

Notes:

_____

_____

_____

_____

_____

_____

_____

_____

_____

_____

_____

_____

_____

_____

_____

_____

_____

_____

_____

_____

_____

ABOUT THE AUTHOR

CONNIE SPARKS

Connie Sparks is president of the Wade Institute, a training organization focusing on women's issues. She has designed workshops presented throughout California and attended by individuals from various nonprofit and for profit organizations.

An expert on women's issues and grant writing, Ms. Sparks is certified and has trained hundreds of individuals venturing into and maintaining a consulting business that relates to professional development and life skills.

Ms. Sparks has worked with women's organizations on developing and implementing support groups to assist women in dealing with violence and abuse. She has conducted workshops on self-empowerment, dealing with low self-esteem, personal development and life skills.

Her grant writing and program development experience encompasses five years for non-profit organizations and public education, having raised more than $2,052,000 to date. In addition to writing grants, her background includes more than nine years in management, program development and human resources, collectively.

Ms. Sparks has had the opportunity to reach and assist dozens of non-profit organizations through her training workshops and consultation services. She's the author of *The Nuts & Bolts of Grant Writing*, an easy- to- read workbook designed to help other grant writers and organizations understand the processes and fundamentals of writing grants and soliciting funds from donors.

Connie Sparks is an active member of the American Parliamentary Institute (API), Toastmasters International, National Association of Female Executives (NAFE), The Professional Woman Network (PWN) and American Business Women Association (ABWA).

Her education includes a degree in Business Management, Certified Diversity Management Instructor and she holds a credential in Business Communication and Computer Applications.

THIRTEEN

SISTA'S AGAINST SISTA'S: HOW TO OVERCOME ENVY

By Connie Sparks

Sista's, have you ever said to yourself, "What does she have that I don't?" "She thinks she's cute!" "Who does she think she is?" or "She ain't all that!" This is a tell-tell sign that you are suffering from a condition called "ENVY".

What is envy? It is defined as, "To feel displeasure and ill will at the superiority of another person in happiness, success, reputation, or the possession of anything desirable." There are different types of envy, healthy envy and unhealthy, and there are two domains of envy, the ego domain of envy and the non-ego domain of envy. In the ego domain of envy, your envy is related to how you view yourself, while in the non-ego domain of envy your envy is not related to how you view yourself. (*Envy*, Dr. Windy Dryden). In this chapter I will be helping you to overcome unhealthy envy and to experience healthy envy.

Envy is commonplace in our time today. Women who have not achieved or acquired their desires in life such as a nice car, big house, a fine husband, or a top paying job, oftentimes envy those women who have successfully achieved these things and seem to have it all together. Why should you envy the woman who has everything? Why not turn that negative emotion into something positive? It's not healthy to tear another woman down to make yourself feel better. The Bible says that envy is "the rottenness of the bones". (Proverbs 14:30). God also says, "Love does not envy." (1 Corinthians 13:4, New King James Version).

I worked for an educational organization for eight years, and during the last two years of my employment I encountered tongue lashes, backstabbing, and vindictive treatments from several women who worked in my department. Out of the eighteen women in the department, the ages ranged from thirties to early sixties, and I was the youngest. I was in my early thirties and was vivacious, ambitious, assertive, young and quite attractive (if I might say so) -- one too many strikes against me (according to the older women). Flaunting wasn't my nature. Although I knew I had a lot going for myself, I didn't have the desire to throw my assets around and let everyone know, "Hey, I'm here! Call me she-woman." My spirit was loving and carefree, always looking to help and support the other woman.

I knew my work performance would speak for itself. You see, it wasn't in my character to make other women feel inferior to me or jealous. In fact, I tried to empower some of the more passive women who lacked certain skills and training, and were not confident in their jobs. I gave them solutions and options that would make their jobs easier and fulfilling. In return for my goodwill, do you know what I got? A big slap in the face! These very women I spent hours helping and encouraging for the better were initiated into the "Jealous Woman's

Club". This was a group of older women who despised younger women, and made it their life's mission to make our lives a living hell.

To make a long story short, they succeeded at tearing me down and making my days miserable. Eventually, I had to take a medical leave of absent for a few months (related to stress) to gain my self-control and rebuild what I allowed them to destroy. When I returned from my medical leave, there had been a lot of new changes (a new director for starters). Also, my job duties had been split between two new employees, which meant that there wasn't anything left for me to do. This was all part of the "Jealous Woman's Club" plot to ease me out of the school district. Well, one day the new director called me into her office and we talked for hours. She shared some things with me that the other women had told her about me. Now mind you she had never met me before my return from medical leave; she only new what had been told to her by other employees in the office. By this time the director had already developed a preconceived notion about me and my character. So, while we were sitting in her office talking, she stopped me in the middle of a sentence and said, "You're nothing like what they described to me." I said, "Excuse me?" She was told that I wasn't a team player, was self-centered, and I didn't know what I was doing. The gossip also stated that I refused to help other co-workers in time of need. This was all about envy! She apologized to me for allowing these women to manipulate her into thinking I was a worthless employee who didn't deserve to be in the department, when in fact it was just the opposite. That was one of the most enlightening conversations I have ever had with a boss on a more personal level. From that conversation she gave me a sound piece of wisdom that would change my life and how I viewed other women who are different from me. She said, ***"You don't have to blow out someone else's candle to make yours shine."***

Although, I wasn't the one blowing out anyone's candle, I took this wisdom and created a framed poster, which I still display to this day and share with women who are caught up in the envy syndrome.

The act described was unhealthy envy. To tear down a woman's joy and success demonstrates shortfalls and insecurities on another woman's part. Recognizing your insecurities, ignorance and failures will enable you to recognize how you can benefit by improving flawed characters. Do you know all your characteristics? Do you know what makes you envious of other women?

Who is the envious woman?

- A perfectionist, driven to do the right thing. Often critical of self as well as others.

- A helper, needing to be needed.

- Wants to be successful in life but is too afraid to take the risks.

- A shallow woman who won't empower another woman, because she is afraid the other woman will out-shine her.

- An individualist, craving self-expression and emotional depth. Sensitive to beauty and meaning, but prone to melancholy, feelings of inadequacy, and envy.

- Full of contradictions which create self-doubt and indecisiveness.

- Insecure, bitter and vindictive.

These are the characteristics of a woman who portrays attributes of unhealthy envy. Unhealthy may be described as an unhealthy feeling that causes many women to bury the realistic side of themselves in a subconscious state, preventing personal development and growth. It's unfortunate that women are suppressed with such a condition, a condition that drives women apart from one another, hence depleting the many contributions we as women can share amongst each other thus creating unity.

The Keys to Overcoming the Stumbling Blocks of Envy

Now that we've established the definition of *envy* and the various effects it has on women, let's discuss solutions and what it will take to overcome *envy*.

The keys include:

1. Dealing with envy

2. Recognizing the change

3. The new you

#1 Dealing With Envy:

As you have learned, envy appears in many forms such as jealousy, which causes women to act in a conniving, deceitful and misbehaving manner. Then there's the unhealthy act of "LUST" (lusting over what another woman has); this is where you commence to verbally tear her down. Did you know that 85% of the time when you hate another woman, and are walking around with a chip on your shoulder, she isn't even aware of how you feel? This means you are wasting all your energy, time and efforts making *yourself* angry.

- ***Dealing with envy*** - You must first recognize and admit that you are an envious woman. Admitting your flaws doesn't necessarily mean that you have low self-esteem or are incapable of empowering other women, but that you have unfulfilled desires waiting for you. Look deep within yourself and allow the considerate and giving character you have within yourself to express itself. Don't allow your selfish emotions to take control.

- ***Confronting your envy*** - Ask yourself, why am I jealous of her? What am I gaining when I discredit or belittle her? What does this say about me? How would I feel if another woman treated me this way? These are key questions you should ask yourself whenever you're in the same circle with the woman you envy. Tell yourself, "I am worthy. I can do and have anything I desire." Don't say, "I can have what she has." You should never want what another woman has. Always strive to have something more for yourself, because you are worth so much more. You have to redirect that negative attitude into something positive by challenging yourself, and give her a compliment when you see her. (Even if you're not able to physically/verbally compliment her, for your own edification mentally give her a compliment!) Say the words to yourself ("She's beautiful." " I love that dress she's wearing."), and over a period of time this process will become more natural to you.

- ***Challenging your abilities*** - Each day make an effort to empower another woman, offer a positive gesture, and/or give her an uplifting compliment. Think about it sista's! We are one of the same, and when one woman excels and achieves a level of success, this is a reflection on all women.

#2 Recognizing the Change:

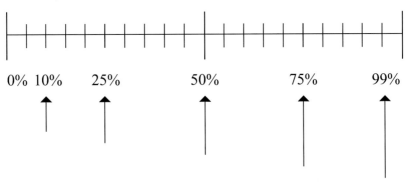

0% 10%   25%   50%   75%   99%

Confront the issue

   Have confidence in yourself

      Define confidence in your needs

         Able to empower other women

            Confidently respect other women

One of the most rewarding feelings is that of achievement; setting measurable goals that you can accomplish will make you a much better person. At first it may not seem like you're making any progress. It's always difficult to spot the day-to-day change, though we look for the change. It's just like dieting, because every day you look at yourself in the mirror to see if there's any change in your figure (or you may step on the scale to see if you've lost any weight), and oftentimes it appears that you have lost nothing. Eventually you become discouraged and lose faith in the diet, but you continue to diet anyway, hoping that in two weeks you'll see a change.

You may be going about your day-to-day chores and your mind has changed its focus onto something else rather than the diet; you are wondering what to wear to your girlfriend's party and voila! You pull out your beautiful, bright red (killer!) dress. You try it on and WOW! It fits! Your diet paid off, even though you couldn't physically see the change. If you apply the same method to overcoming your envy, you will begin to see a change within yourself that will be rewarding and uplifting.

- *Confronting the Issue* - Confronting the issue is dealing with the inner you and admitting you have a problem with envy. If you remain in denial about your situation, it is less likely you will be able to overcome the condition and grow into the flourishing, beautiful and confident woman that you are.

- *Building Your Confidence and Character* - Your character is one of the key ingredients to who you are and how you relate to others. As children we develop natural characteristics from our environment and parents. During this growing period, we encounter some negative situations, which subconsciously hinder us from developing the key characteristics that affect our confidence. Perhaps it was a family member or schoolmate that said something to you, which made you feel uncomfortable or ashamed. (Take a few minutes and think about what hurtful or negative things that were said to you which may have possibly made you lose confidence in yourself.) Maybe someone said, "You won't be worth anything!" "She's prettier than you," (comparing you to another young lady), or "No one will ever marry you!" These are all degrading, demeaning and scornful words used to emotionally strip a woman of her self-worth and self-respect. Moreover, these words can also be used to make you stronger and determined to prove that person wrong!

- *Defining Confidence in Your Needs* - We're going to take those **lemons** and turn them into **lemonade**. Make a list of affirmations (approximately six), which will reflect the positive aspects of the lemons. Say these affirmations to yourself every morning while dressing for work, school or when you're sitting in the car. ("They may have said that I was stupid, but I am going to complete my Masters Degree!" "I deserve success because I have worked hard and am worthy.") When you recite the affirmations, you should be looking into a mirror with a big and beautiful smile. I guarantee you will be uplifted and feel more confident about who you are and what you can accomplish! You will ultimately begin to see the positives that have come from the negatives.

- *Ability To Empower and Respect Other Women - It's* truly a powerful experience when a woman can have the power to enrich the lives of other women through her words of encouragement. At this stage of development you have not only honed your level of confidence (which allows you to freely accept the changes you've made), but you are now in a position to recognize the value in supporting and uplifting other women to be all they can be.

#3 The New You

A woman should never feel inferior to another woman! Instead, she should think of herself as an equal. It doesn't matter how much money, the size of the house, the job title or even the kind of car another woman has! You as a woman are just as important and valuable as the next woman.

As time goes on and you began to feel more confident about yourself and your accomplishments, other women will observe a different you. You will also notice people being drawn to you and wanting to be in your company. That alone will make you feel like you're on top of the world! Take advantage of all the new opportunities that arise, and don't be afraid to take a stance. Go after what you want and feel good about taking another woman with you so that it is a beneficial opportunity for both of you. Remember also that healthy envy is inevitable. You will watch other women rise to the top and that is to be commended. If you feel the need to strive for the same type of goal, then go for it! Just don't hold another sista down on your journey up the ladder. Bring her up, too!

There's nothing like having other positive and confident women in your circle creating a pathway for success. Envy has no place in the hearts of women, it can destroy a woman's value and self-pride, inhibiting her from the many opportunities life has to offer. Don't allow this obstacle to prevent you from enjoying the luxuries of being in the company of successful women *who are not filled with envy* and whom you can admire without feeling envious or unsure of yourself.

"Envy is not a woman's right, it is a hindering flaw that will either break us or make us stronger."
— Connie Sparks

Notes:

ABOUT THE AUTHOR

SUZETTE SALANDY

Suzette Salandy, a native of the beautiful island of Trinidad, has been working in public relations and human resources for over eleven years. Also, since 1997, Suzette has been working as a Professional Image Consultant specializing in multi-occasion make-up artistry. Suzette's philanthropic interests have enabled her to donate her time and talents to many charitable organizations, including Dress for Success, a not-for-profit organization dedicated to helping underprivileged women succeed in the work force. As an image consultant, she conducts individual consultation sessions helping women improve their self-presentation and makeup/grooming habits, and has successfully led several workshops helping teen mothers enhance their image and professionalism in the workplace.

Suzette, a member of the Society of Human Resource Management and the National Association for Female Executives, has recently been appointed to the International Advisory Board for The Professional Woman Network. Suzette loves to travel and her philosophy is dream it, do it!

Suzette Salandy is a co-author of *Customer Service & Professionalism for Women* in the PWN library.

Contact:
Salandy Consulting
590 Edbridge Road
Morrisville, PA 19067
(215) 313-0242
S90971@aol.com
www.protrain.net

FOURTEEN

HEALTH AND WELLNESS: MIND, BODY & SPIRIT

By Suzette Salandy

T he Wake up Call

I remember the day my former husband told me that he was diagnosed with colon cancer. It was October 2004. As he shared the news about having stage-four colon rectal cancer, I remember the fear I felt in my heart, but I never showed Dane my fear. Instead, I supported him in his fight. Dane maintained he would kick this disease and, given that he was an avid soccer player and believed in eating a healthy diet, he continued to fight the battle. This was a siren that echoed for many of us in the family as we all conducted colon cancer screening, along with other types of physical screening based on family history. For two and a half years, Dane fought his fight against cancer, but in January 2006, he lost the battle. I shared this story with you because it was my own wake up call regarding my health. It became clear to me that my health and well-being was not just about scheduling time to exercise and doing occasional diets but instead, it is a lifelong journey.

Mind, Body & Spirit

The journey to wellness starts with the mind. A strong spiritual connection helps us to maintain a balance within our lives. The mind is instrumental in preventing stress and anxiety within the body. Think of the body as a temple and the mind as the source that governs every movement within the temple. The term "your spirit is willing but the flesh is weak," stems from the lack of brainpower that gets the body moving. Your state of wellness starts with your thoughts.

One of the best methods of relaxation and exercise is yoga. It's an ancient art based on balancing the body, mind and spirit. The continued practice of yoga is great as it strengthens the body and serves as a source of emotional stability and clarity of mind. Yoga is one of the best de-stressors that we can use in our day-to-day life. Yoga also incorporates meditation, allowing us to reduce tension and find calmness within ourselves. Another simple form of stress release is deep breathing; taking deep breaths a few seconds to a few minutes a day helps to alleviate the anxiety. For example, if you are feeling anger and frustration, take a few deep breaths. Also, the art of positive thinking is important. Saying an encouraging affirmation every day gives you the feeling of accomplishment and allows you to be more focused on the good aspects of your life.

Why are mind, body and spirit important? Stress can trigger unhealthy reactions and these may contribute to overeating, which leads to possible overweight; being overweight can result in diabetes, hypertension and other stress-related diseases. As you can see, it is vital to reduce stress in your life; the mind impacts the body and the body impacts the mind. Never forget this.

Movement

One of the greatest myths about exercise is that it is difficult. Getting healthy can be as simple as a walk in the park. One of my greatest joys in the morning is having that ten-minute walk with my dog, Bailey. I maintain a busy schedule and cannot always go to the gym to exercise, but I welcome those few minutes in the morning when my body is being rejuvenated by the fresh air, and it gives me the opportunity to enjoy the solitude and peace of my thoughts.

So many of us think that exercise requires a rigorous schedule, but if you are unable to plan that gym time, then take just a few minutes each day and incorporate movement. Take the stairs instead of the elevator, spend some time in the park with your children, or ride a bike on the weekends. If thirty minutes a day for working out is not feasible, then break it down into three manageable ten-minute intervals throughout the day. My all- time favorite form of movement is dancing. I love dancing and often incorporate dancing in my workout. From time to time, I seek out some of my dear friends and we go out dancing. Cardiovascular movements are extremely important for the heart.

For those of you who get bored with your workout routine, its time to revamp your routine. Here are some suggestions: swimming is a great overall body workout; it not only is cardiovascular, but it also tones the muscles. Pilates is another good form of exercise and is similar to yoga. It has an element of mind-body discipline and is a great physical workout. Tai-Chi is another optional workout; it structures deep breathing with movement and muscle relaxation. Studies have found that many of these movements can reduce and manage anxiety, headaches, hypertension, and even asthma. Remember, if you are short on time, small spurts of exercise can relieve stress and shape your body. Also, reward yourself after a workout. There is nothing like a shiatsu massage or a hot stone deep tissue massage. Some studies show that a massage releases endorphins, which are brain chemicals that elevate mood and weaken pain. If you can't afford a full body massage, then try a 15-30 minute chair massage to relax. While there is no price tag on good health, the best part of these exercise routines is they can be very inexpensive. Most of your local YMCA locations offer classes at a minimal cost.

Nutrition

Fruits and vegetables are an essential part of our daily intake. The fresher your fruits and vegetables, the better the taste. The key to grocery shopping is adding a variety of new foods to your daily intake, which will allow you to expand your food palate. I love mangoes and find that every summer I look forward to having at least one or two mangoes a day. Mangoes are very low in saturated fat, cholesterol and sodium. They are also a good source of dietary fiber and Vitamin B6, Vitamin A and Vitamin C. Having lived on a tropical island for most of my life, I find that fruits such as mangoes, pineapples, kiwis and watermelons add such a great difference to my overall nutritional intake.

While an apple a day keeps the doctor away, many of the other fruits have great nutritional value as well. Try eating a kiwi. They are a good source of potassium, magnesium and have twice the Vitamin C content than that of an orange. Top awards go to the guava and papaya; they are both high in Vitamin C content. Guava is rich in fiber, which helps prevent constipation, and papaya is rich in carotene, which is good for your eyes. Orange and green vegetables contain an antidote known as beta-carotene—a form of Vitamin A, which helps to fight cancer. A favorite vegetable is broccoli. It's very easy to steam and microwaves very well. One recommended tip is to avoid garnishing broccoli with fatty cheeses and creams. Instead, try some lemon juice or add some flavorful seasonings. I love my grandmother's recipe, and throughout the years, I realized that many of her ingredients were high in flavor without a lot of fat and sodium. The key to preparing most of your meals is finding seasonings that can give the food a good taste, but does not consist of high sodium content. There are some great substitutes for salt, such as lemon pepper, cilantro, or Mrs. Dash seasonings. Studies have shown that hypertension occurs in one of every three African-American women.

Whole grains and fibers are also essential to our nutritional plan. Whole wheat breads and cereals are a good source of B-complex vitamins, including folate (folic acid), and have many important minerals such as iron, magnesium, copper, phosphorus and zinc, and a good source of antioxidants, including vitamin E and selenium, which can help lower blood cholesterol levels and help to fight against breast cancer.

The Reality

It's natural to dream big. We all want to lose weight and fit back into those college jeans, but setting such high goals makes it difficult when you fail to achieve them. Instead, take small steps to improve your health, and build on each day as you improve. Remember that it's okay to still have some of your favorite foods and desserts, but you can learn to substitute a few of the ingredients. When eating in restaurants, don't eat all the portions; instead make an effort to eat less portions. There is an ancient Greek myth that says, "Rome was not built in a day." The process of improving your eating takes time. For example: my schedule is crazy from day to day so, to avoid getting overwhelmed, I try to create meals that are simple, easy and healthy. My son, Ryan loves pizza, and I make home made pizzas quite often using low-fat cheese and other more healthy ingredients, and he loves them.

Family History

My grandmother made some wonderful cakes and pies, but she could not enjoy all of her wonderful baking because she had diabetes. I'm part of a generation that has hypertension and diabetes, so getting tested every year for both is mandatory in my health screenings. Knowing your family history is very important to your health and wellness. Talk to your parents and ask not only about their health, but that of their parents. Oftentimes, diseases may skip a generation, so it's important to know your entire history. I also recommend that when you visit your health practitioner, know not just your height and weight, but also your blood pressure, cholesterol and blood glucose numbers. Keeping track of those numbers will help to reduce the risk of heart disease and stroke.

The Woman in the Mirror

The beauty and versatility of black skin is wonderful. We vary in skin tones, but while our pigmentation may be different from those of our Caucasian counterparts, we must still be vigilant about checking our skin for skin cancer. Have any mole or mark checked by your dermatologist for diagnosis and treatment. Remember as we look in the mirror, that beauty exudes not just on the outside, but also on the inside. Continue your journey of health and wellness, uplift your mind, body and spirit, and know that we are all beautiful and wonderful human beings, and should treat ourselves as the queens we are and deserve to be.

I miss my best friend, Dane, each and every day of my life, but I know that he is in a much better place—a place of beauty where there is no pain and suffering. I am grateful for the time that I spent with him, and more importantly for the gift he gave me, the gift of a healthier life.

1. Are you aware of your family medical history?

2. Do you visit your doctor for annual physicals and related screenings?

3. How often to you conduct self-breast examinations?

4. Is movement a part of your daily routine?

5. What challenges do you experience, when trying to conduct a good nutritional and exercise plan?

6. What steps have you taken to overcome some of the challenges?

7. Do you often revamp your daily exercise routine?

8. How would you rate your overall eating and exercise plan on a scale of 1-10, with 10 being the highest?

9. Do you often feel anxious and overwhelmed by some of your daily tasks?

10. How often do you take time to relax and or meditate?

Recommended Tips

1. Take a few minutes each day and record a list of some of the foods that you eat during breakfast, lunch and or dinner. Keep the list for approximately two weeks. On the third week, try changing some of the foods and replacing it with something healthy but different that you may not have ever eaten, but was curious to try.

2. Write an affirmation about something positive in your life, and place it where you can have the opportunity to see and read everyday.

May you be blessed on your journey to better health. Be ever mindful of your spiritual, mental and physical needs. Take time for yourself always, and fill your mind with good thoughts, your body with healthy foods, and your spirit with God's word, and His desire for you to be a wonderfully healthy African-American woman who treats her body like the temple that it is.

Notes:

ABOUT THE AUTHOR

Kamala C. McGee

Kamala C. McGee is currently working as a nurse for a major healthcare organization. She is a twenty-six year veteran of the U.S. Military, in which she has held numerous leadership and management positions. Kamala holds an Associate degree in nursing, a Bachelor's degree in Psychology and is currently working towards a dual Master's degree in Nursing/Business Administration/Healthcare.

Kamala McGee has been certified in Diversity and Wellness Issues by The Professional Woman Network and has also been trained as an Equal Opportunity Representative (EOA), Consideration of Others Facilitator, and Critical Incident Stress Management (CISM).

She wishes to be a guide to assist women in identifying their strengths and weaknesses, assist the youth of today in reaching their potential, and be beneficial in improving the communication gap amongst all in society. Kamala also wishes to thank all those who have touched her life for a season and the lessons taught and learned.

Contact:
Kamala C. McGee
PO Box 3607
Danville, VA 24543
434.797.4932/434.770.0007
kamichar@earthlink.net
www.protrain.net

FIFTEEN

SISTER, TO THINE OWN SELF BE TRUE! KNOW YOUR VALUES

By Kamala C. McGee

Our lives can often be told in stories, plays, song, and poetry (or a combination of them all). How it is played out depends upon our perceptions of self and the decisions we make. In the story following, you may see yourself, or you may know someone who has experienced (or is experiencing) some of the trials depicted.

Imagine it is a breezy, balmy afternoon and you have just arrived home from a long day at work, school or other activity. You live in a quiet neighborhood with your mother, husband, significant other, children, or other family members. Everyone is presently out of the house, which gives you time to relax, meditate, reflect on the life and path you have walked over the years. A path that has been filled with sunshine, rain, and at times very divided and conflicted.

In your processing, you are always trying to please everyone around you, taking on their problems and circumstances as your own and giving so much to others emotionally, mentally, physically, and financially that you have lost your own identity. Why? Because you have a subconscious force that pushes you to believe that it is your responsibility—a means to 'atone' for your mistakes and choices. It is a subconscious force, so strong that it convinces you that you have to accept the treatment or maltreatment from those individuals you have allowed to enter into your space and be of service to.

In your reflecting, you have discovered that there are many scenes in your life that have pushed you to the water's edge; holding you hostage. This allows your space continuously to be filled and invaded by people, situations, and circumstances from which you need to be set free. You begin to search and evaluate your life, looking for a particular catalyst and reason for the choices and decisions you have made and continue to make. What could this catalyst be?

1. Perhaps it is the relationship that you either have or do not have with your mother or father. A relationship in which you are seeking the love, acceptance, acknowledgement, and respect that you feel is so desperately missing. Never hearing your father say, "You are my daughter," or "I love you and am proud of you." Perhaps you have met him only twice in your life and are left with so many unanswered questions.

2. During your search and reflections, you discover that you have allowed yourself to get involved in various relationships and

friendships that leave you questioning your purpose, your existence, and the desire you have to punish yourself for not being worthy or good enough to have someone in your life to really care and support you. In these relationships, the individuals are only there long enough to obtain their goals or meet their needs, and then walk out leaving you with a bag filled with emptiness.

3. Maybe it was the relationship in which you became pregnant and you chose to have and raise your baby alone, or you placed the baby up for adoption, or possibly you chose another alternative—abortion. (Can you imagine the emotional, psychological, physical consequences?)

Either way, the choices you make or made are dependent on your idea of what you thought was the best thing for you, and your ideas about self and the things you may or may not deserve. Emotionally you carry the baggage of a multitude of suppressed feelings. You are unable to tell anyone how your feel or what you did because you fear their judgment and rejection. You learn to internalize all the negative emotions that surround you, pretending that all is well with you, hoping that you do not have to face, revisit, or acknowledge your true self. You struggle with yourself about how to feel, whether to feel, and with the validity of your feelings. So, what would happen if you chose to allow your emotions to manifest? You are afraid that the strength of your emotions will be so much that you crumble under the weight of it all. On the other hand, perhaps you will be lost in the darkness, afraid to face yourself and afraid to move forward. Oh, the void that hides in the recesses of your soul.

Self-Truth

> *"You can out-distance that which is running after you,*
> *but not what is inside of you."*
> —Rwandan Proverb

One beautiful sunlit day you awaken to the realization that you have been running and hiding from your 'true self', the inner voice that so softly speaks, jolting you into actually facing the mirror and acknowledging all that is there. This same small voice urges and cajoles you into accepting and believing that you are something special, something so divinely created with a wealth of untapped potential and a destiny to fulfill. However, it first must begin with you really evaluating all the steps on the path you have walked. You must acknowledge and confront the self that harbors the hurt, anger, sadness, frustration, guilt and other self-defeating mantras that are holding you hostage. Yes, it is a frightening thought to begin looking into the mirror and see your true self. But there comes a time when we must first face all that we are in order to become all that we are suppose to be. Look into the 'eyes of a soul' and embrace the divine spirit within.

Eyes of a Soul

If you look into the eyes,
Eyes of a soul
What you may see within -
A vulnerable spirit trying to defend
The loneliness, anger, and hurt
That cannot be expressed
For it leaves the spirit

Open and undressed.
But with patience, understanding
And a just a little time
You may witness the blossoming
Of a wondrous design.
So when looking into the eyes
Eyes of a Soul
Look with your heart
And God's gift you will behold –
"You"
— Kamala C. McGee

Therefore, sisters, becoming true to thy self is a process of purpose, growth, and understanding. One must first have understanding and insight into the definition of self-truth. Self-truth is the essence of our actions, beliefs and thoughts that are fruits born of our life experiences and the choices made thereto. Virginia Woolf once said, "If you do not tell the truth about yourself, you cannot tell it about other people." Moreover, as the poem states, you have to look into the eyes of your soul and identify yourself. The five questions below will be helpful in guiding you on your journey to self-discovery.

Exercise

1. Who do you say you are? Identify five or more character traits that you possess.

_____   _____
_____   _____
_____   _____
_____   _____
_____   _____

2. Every story of play has a theme. What is your life's theme? How is it reflective of your self-truth?

_____
_____
_____
_____
_____

3. Emotionally or spiritually, have you struggled with finding your way? How might you be able to find your direction?

_____
_____
_____
_____
_____

4. What are some ways or techniques that you can use to enhance your self-truth?

_____

_____

_____

_____

_____

_____

5. Can, you trust yourself? Why or why not?

_____

_____

_____

_____

_____

_____

"To thine own self be true, and it must follow, as the night the day, there canst not then be false to any man." — William Shakespeare

Values

When you complete the task of identifying yourself and acknowledging and embracing all that it encompasses, then it becomes more apparent in our actions, behaviors, and especially our values. Our values are associated components of our self-truth. They are the outline provided us by our parents that evolve into the foundation on which "Self" develops. How we see the glass, either half- empty or half- full, affects the view that we show the world and ourselves.

No one can tell you which values you should adopt as your own. Some things are learned from parents, peers, life experience, or innate to us and housed in the conscience, "that still small voice that is sometimes too loud for comfort." – Bert Murray. Values vary from individual to individual, but below is a list of six values that you or other individuals may hold dear:

1. **God** or other Spiritual Leader

   – The entity of divine creation and existence

2. **Self**

   – The whole of who you are or will become

3. **Faith**

   – "If ye have faith as a grain of mustard seed." – Matt 17:20

   – A grain is so miniscule, yet grows so wondrously

4. **Heart** – The center of the soul

   – "Search me, O God and know my heart; try me and know my thought." – Ps. 139:23

   – For as he thinketh in his heart, so is he." – Prov. 23:7

5. **Hope** – The foundation of dreams

   – "Hope deferred maketh the heart sick, but when the desire cometh, it is a tree of life." – Prov. 13:12

6. **Love** – Sacrifice

   – "There is no fear in love; but perfect love casteth out fear; because fear hath torment. He that feareth is not perfect in love." – 1 John 4:18

Make a list of your values and identify why they are important to you. Also, is this list incumbent of what you present to yourself and others?

_____

_____

_____

_____

_____

_____

_____

_____

_____

_____

In your journey, you must know that there is a higher power in your life that has created you for a divine purpose. In addition, know that through your faith all things are possible; in your heart you hold the key to self-discovery, in hope you can see your visions, and in love you can discover yourself. There will be times when you will question the things that are happening in your life, but the beacon that you see in the far off distance is the light for your path. Here is another quote I wish to share that is very reflective of how embracing one's self-truths and values can lead to a more fulfilled life and understanding:

"Trust yourself. Create the kind of self that you will be happy to live with all your life. Make the most of yourself by fanning the tiny inner sparks of possibility into flaming achievements."- Foster C.

McClellan. Perhaps the next time you look into the 'eyes of a soul' you will encounter

The Twinkle In My Eye
The new little twinkle in my eyes
The brand new pep in my step
The way I hold my head high
Every chance I get
Is it a man you ask?
A new love maybe
I say, it's the power of the women surrounding me
The pain in their hearts
The joy in their eyes
The release of humanity
In every tear they cry.
I am empowered, influenced and embraced
By every challenge, struggle and fear they've faced
Joined together our hearts as one.
Whatever's to become of us
Already has been done.
What more can we take?
What more can we say?
There's nothing left to do but kneel and pray
Awakened by a new day
With hope in our eyes.
It's got to get better
The Lord's heard our cries.
A new beginning, an understanding no doubt
Of what this life's really about.

I got it now; I didn't before
The sassy attitude that men adore.
What is the wonder?
What is it they see?
A reflection of strength staring back at me.
I chose to listen and not ignore
The struggle and strife no man can endure.
Beauty's what's left, sincerity and pride
And now you understand the new twinkle in my eye.
— Charlene Steele – AKA "Shay"

Remember, God entrusts you with yourself. BE BLESSED!! Moreover, find inspiration in all that you do and encounter.

References

The Holy Bible: Old and New Testaments. (2003). (King James Version).

Thomas Nelson Bibles: New York

http://www.inspirational-quotes.com

Recommended Reading

1. *Can You Stand to be Blessed?* by T.D. Jakes

2. *Celebrate the Journey* by Debra Fulghum-Bruce & Ellen Oldacre

3. *One Day My Soul Just Opened Up* by Iyanla Vanzant

4. *10 Spiritual Principles of Successful Women* by Victoria Lowe

5. *The Purpose Driven Life* by Rick Warren

ABOUT THE AUTHOR

DR. MAMIE SHIELDS NORMAN

Dr. Mamie Shields Norman is the library media specialist and technology coordinator at Thomas Johnson Middle School in Lanham, Maryland, Prince George's County Public Schools. She serves as adjunct faculty at Sojourner-Douglass College in Annapolis, Maryland, and is the owner/CEO of The Shields Group, LLC, an educational and personal development consulting firm.

Dr. Shields Norman owns and operates a pre-K Montessori weekend school. She has presented various workshops on early childhood and independence in the very young child. During 2004 Dr. Norman was a presenter at the Professional Woman Network International Conference in Louisville, Kentucky, and served on the 2005 Woman Network International Advisory Board.

Before returning to the library profession, Dr. Shields Norman taught pre-K Montessori for eight years. She has been an educator for 38 years and is committed to the education of children, youth and adults, encouraging them to reach their highest potential and become all they can be.

Certification in the following areas qualifies Dr. Shields Norman to be of great service to many: Leadership Skills for Women, Becoming the Assertive Woman, Self-esteem and Self-empowerment, pre-K Montessori, and Anger Management for Young People.

Dr. Sheilds Norman is a native of Memphis Tennessee and the sixth child of seven. She currently resides in Bowie, Maryland with her two sons, Yohance and Zikomo. Dr. Shields Norman holds a Bachelor's degree in Sociology form Tuskegee University, a Master's in Library Science from Atlanta University, a Master's in Elementary Education from American International College, a Master's in Guidance and Psychological Services from Springfield College, and is AMI-certified as pre-K Montessori. She is currently awaiting the conferment of her Doctorate of Education from NOVA Southeastern University.

Contact:
The Shields Group, LLC
15480 Annapolis Road Ste. 202 #258
Bowie, MD 20715
mshields2@verizon.net
www.protrain.net

SIXTEEN

WALKING ON YOUR SPIRITUAL JOURNEY

By Dr. Mamie Shields Norman

Walking on your spiritual journey is very important in your life on Earth. It is all about your soul's salvation, and your soul is the essence of your being. So, getting in touch with your soul (your mind—yourself) is vital to your peace, joy, happiness, fulfillment, discovering your purpose on Earth, and walking in your purpose every day. Walking on your spiritual journey is walking in the "Fruit of the Spirit". What is the "Fruit of the Spirit"? "The Fruit of the Spirit is love, joy, peace, longsuffering, gentleness, goodness, meekness, temperance and kindness." So, as you walk on your spiritual journey, you are seeking for those things up above which are everlasting. We need to expand our desire to know our Creator and let the Light of God shine through us. Walking on our spiritual journey will allow us to receive more of God's presence in our lives; receive more knowledge of God, receive more spiritual feelings. On the other hand, we are not walking on our spiritual journey when we are seeking those things of the Earth, which will pass away and are only temporary.

Ask yourself this question, "Am I seeking material things or am I seeking spiritual maturity?" Bare in mind that our spiritual journey starts from within, and is not an outward appearance by which another human may judge us as spiritual or not. Our spiritual journey and seeking material gain cannot co-exist. If we are sincere about our spiritual journey, then materialism will be of no importance!

If we take a close look at the Earth's population, we will find that most of us have a strong desire for earthly things and material desire for the basic essentials. (There are also a number of people who will give up their soul's salvation to be rich. They seek only wealth and spend their whole lives seeking money.) The third group of people are seekers of power, status, positions in the company, power and control over others. The fourth group are seekers of knowledge, new discoveries, and are a group of people on Earth seeking the spiritual kingdom of God and things up above.

Have you ever asked soul-searching questions such as:

• Who am I?

• Where did I come from?

• Why was I born?

• Where am I going?

• Have I been here on Earth before?

• Why is there so much chaos and suffering in the world?

- How can we stop the suffering and chaos?

- How can I obtain complete fulfillment, peace, joy, and happiness every day of my life?

- How long will I exist on Earth?

- What will my life be like once I leave Earth?

- Will my life continue as it is when I reach the other side?

- Am I a spiritual being?

These, and many similar questions, are asked by each of us at some point in time during our life. We do not have the answers to all of them, and probably will not until we reach the spiritual "perfection" maturity. How do we reach spiritual "perfection" maturity? First, we "*must walk in love, as Christ also has loved us.*" We must "*walk as children of light and in the fruit of the Spirit.*" As the scripture states, "*Be ye perfect as your Father in Heaven is perfect.*" (That is, perfect in our daily walk on our spiritual journey.) Up to this point there has been only one perfect being who has walked planet Earth and that is Jesus Christ, our Lord and Savior.

So you are probably saying, "How can I walk my spiritual journey like Jesus?" Very easily! Just accept Jesus Christ as your Lord and Savior, and turn your life over to God through Jesus. Simple! You see, we are so busy with life and focusing on the things of the world like money, fame, fortune, houses, cars, clothes, status, etc. (all those things which will pass away), rather than focusing on the things up above which are eternal and which guarantee us the success, peace, joy, happiness, and fruit of the spiritual.

Now this is not to say that God does not want us to enjoy our material objects and personal successes. He surely does or He would not have made things possible for us to discover. All He wants us to do is to put Him first on our spiritual journey and He will make the road easy. We can accept the challenges, chaos, conflicts, and bad relationships with the attitude of the Fruit of the Spirit. We will understand that underneath all the hard aches, pains, suffering, losses, challenges, and hurts, that there is joy – the inward stability which keeps us going and going and going like the energized "bunny". We can do all that is ordained for us with joy in our hearts, knowing that all that we do, we do as unto the Lord.

God, Himself, has a plan for each of our lives. Our responsibility is to seek and find the plan He has for us. God knows the end of all and the beginning of all. Again, it is our walk on our spiritual journey, which will lead us to God's plan for each of us. Rest assured that each of us has a separate plan. It is up to us to discover God's plan for our individual lives. Walking on your spiritual journey will help one discover this plan.

When we were younger, we may have asked our parents, teachers, pastors, friends, neighbors or anyone whom we thought would have the answers as to our purpose here on Earth. Unfortunately, in most of our educational institutions, we are not trained to continue to ask such questions and seek the answers. So as we mature and become adults these questions resurface, and we once again begin to seek the answers. It is obvious from the sales of self-help books that people are seeking ways to understand themselves better. More and more people are visiting bookstores to learn about themselves, and perhaps a clear picture as to their purpose in life. For some, they are so busy that they never have the time to do personal "soul searching". Many people get so busy with life, school, college, marriage, children, taking care of homes, cars, going to work, dealing with life issues in local communities, and the endless fast-track of life, that they stop asking these vital questions.

Asking these questions and seeking their answers and meaning is the essence of walking on your spiritual journey. You ask, how could this be so? What role do we play in helping return to the state of harmony and peace as it was in the beginning? This may seem very idealistic, but the peace and harmony *we seek* is fulfilling unto itself, and truly allows us to enjoy each and every day. We can learn to experience a day of peace, joy, happiness, sharing, and loving each other without conditions. When we return to a state of peace and harmony, we are free to be who we are meant to be: a loving, giving, kind, patient, compassionate individual. We are made in the image of God and God has all of these qualities, which He placed in us. We have to choose to let the positive qualities rise to the forefront. This is part of walking our spiritual journey and the destination is returning to our Creator. How we walk on this journey is very important in determining how long it will take us to reach our destination or fulfill our mission in life on planet Earth.

As we begin our walk, there are two things we must keep in mind: first, we cannot go back and relive the past. Second, we cannot go forward and live in the future. So, that only leaves the present time, the 'NOW', in which we must learn to walk on our spiritual journey. It is to be a daily walk, which can be vulnerable, fulfilling, challenging, peaceful, joyous, meaningful, loving, long-suffering, and patient. It is a Kingdom Walk!

The following are twelve steps you may want to consider as you prepare, or continue, to walk on your spiritual journey:

- **YOU MUST SPEND TIME WITH GOD, JESUS AND THE HOLY GHOST** each and every day. Make time for them as you make time to prepare for work, clean your home, and take care of your family. Remember Mary and Martha who had a visit to their home by Jesus. Martha was busy cooking and preparing to please Jesus with a good meal and presenting a clean home. But Mary was at the feet of Jesus, listening and learning what she needed to know as she walked on her spiritual journey. Which character would you choose to follow, Mary or Martha? SPEND TIME WITH GOD DAILY.

Select days and times when you will spend special time with God, Jesus and the Holy Ghost. Share your thoughts here:

_____

_____

- **SURROUND YOURSELF WITH OTHERS WHO ARE ON THEIR SPIRITUAL JOURNEY.** Locate friends and groups for support, fellowship, and sharing the love and power of God in your life.

List five people you would like to have fellowship with as you walk your spiritual journey:

1. _____

2. _____

3. _____

4. _____

5. _____

• **CHOOSE YOUR SPIRITUAL PRECEPTS.** Put your precepts into practice in all aspects of your life (not just on Sunday or a religious function). Your spiritual precepts should guide your daily life each and every day. They include how we relate to one another, what we do for each other, how we share and help each other.

List five precepts that you know you can follow on a regular basis:

1. _____

2. _____

3. _____

4. _____

5. _____

• **LOVE ALL BEINGS.** The foundation of life living is based on love. Hate no one, no matter what he or she has done to you, said to you, or spoken about you. You must love all beings. If we say we love God, whom we have never seen, then how can we hate our brothers and sisters whom we see every day! You cannot love God and hate your fellowman. It is as simple as that. It means that you have nothing but love in your heart for all beings and that you care about what happens to them. If you find yourself not holding loving feelings for another person, pray for them daily and lift them up to Jesus.

List five people you dislike and make every effort to love them, in spite of difficulties or relationship issues:

1. _____

2. _____

3. _____

4. _____

5. _____

- **MAKE FRIENDS ALONG YOUR SPIRITUAL JOURNEY.**
  This will help you feel alive and a part of life to witness others on their journeys. Seek love, peace, joy, happiness and fulfillment daily with others. We need one another. No man is an island and no man stands alone.

Make friends with five new people. Invite them to join your support group. Name five people who are potential spiritual friends:

1. _____

2. _____

3. _____

4. _____

5. _____

- **REACH OUT AND HELP SOMEONE WHO NEEDS YOU.** We are here and receive from God for the sake of sharing. Remember that God gave His only begotten Son to save us, to help us. Therefore, reaching out and helping others is a reasonable request. The love and light you receive from God is to be shared with those who are stumbling in the dark and not sure of which way to turn.

Step out on faith and love in your heart and help five people you do not know. Return to this exercise after you have met five strangers to whom you reached out with light and love. Name them here:

1. _____

2. _____

3. _____

4. _____

5. _____

- **DO NOT JUDGE OTHERS.** God is the only judge. How can we be helpful if we are judgmental? "Judge not lest ye be judged."

List five statements of judgment you have directed towards someone you know:

1. _____

2. _____

3. _____

4. _____

5. _____

• **INCREASE YOUR FAITH IN THE POWER OF GOD AND THE POWER OF HIM WORKING IN YOUR LIFE NOW.** Oftentimes we feel that we are alone on this planet, but God is beside you all of the time. He sees all, knows all, and is with everyone all of the time. Be assured that God is dwelling within you and that you are not alone. Turn your life over to Him. It is real and true. He is dwelling within you. Just trust your heart, trust God, and turn your life over to Him.

List five ways that you can increase your faith in the power of God:

1. _____

2. _____

3. _____

4. _____

5. _____

• **RESPECT OTHERS' SPIRITUAL JOURNEYS.** God loves all of us! He loves **all** of human kind. He has outlined a plan or a map for each of us to follow on our journey. We cannot change someone's journey. It is preordained by God.

List five ways that you can show respect for someone else's spiritual journey:

1. _____

2. _____

3. _____

4. _____

5. _____

- **TAKE THE TIME TO BE STILL.** It is in the stillness and quietness that God has a greater opportunity to guide us. We can learn to be quiet and still so that we are able to know what He is trying to say and show us. If we are constantly on the go and keeping busy with life, we are missing God's signals.

   List five things you can do to be still and listen to God:

1. _____

2. _____

3. _____

4. _____

5. _____

• **ALWAYS DO WHAT IS RIGHT.** It is so easy and tempting to do what is wrong, but we must do what we know in our hearts is right. Take a review of the Ten Commandments. If we choose not to follow the commandments and have made a wrong choice, then turn back to God and make the right decision.

List five things that you know, in your heart, would be wrong to do as you are walking on your spiritual journey:

1. _____

2. _____

3. _____

4. _____

5. _____

• **ALWAYS BE THANKFUL FOR EVERYTHING.** We must "*give thanks always for all things unto God and the Father in the name of our Lord Jesus Christ.*" Thankfulness expresses kindness, love and appreciation for what has been done for us.

List five things for which you can be thankful:

1. _____

2. _____

3. _____

4. _____

5. _____

List five people in your life for which you are thankful:

1. _____

2. _____

3. _____

4. _____

5. _____

"Behold, I stand at the door, and knock: If any man hear my voice, and open the door, I will come unto him, and will sup with him, and he with me." When this happens as you walk on your journey, you will become spiritually transformed and become "God's workmanship upon the Earth." *"For we are His workmanship, created in Christ Jesus unto good works, which God hath before ordained that we should walk in them."*

The desire to know and to please God is the goal of walking on your spiritual journey. May you enjoy this walk and journey to the fullest!

ABOUT THE AUTHOR

ANISE KEY BROWN

Anise Key Brown brings more than 20 years of professional experience in human development, transformation and community empowerment. She possesses a Bachelor's degree in Sociology and has received two Master Degrees; one from the State University of New York at Albany and the other from Miami University in Oxford, Ohio. She has pursued post-graduate studies at Howard University in Washington, D.C. and has obtained certifications in Management from the American Management Association. She has also studied at the John F. Kennedy School of Government at Harvard University. She is a certified ESOL (English for Speakers of Other Languages) instructor and an Adult Literacy Tutor.She has received certification as a Life Coach from the Empowerment Institute in Rhinebeck, New York.

Mrs. Brown has worked for the Los Angeles Department of Human Services and tenured as an Assistant Professor for a private University in North Carolina. Her most recent experiences include program development work for an international women's organization in Washington, D.C. where she lobbied on Capitol Hill for issues related to the well-being and empowerment of women from a global perspective. She is the founder of ANISE, Inc. (Anise Newton Institute for Self Empowerment) which is an organization designed to help women realize their full potential in life. She currently serves as the Director of a local government agency in Silver Spring, Maryland.

As a civic activist, Mrs. Brown has held memberships and leadership positions in a number of organizations including the local chapter of the NAACP, the League of Women Voters, the National Political Congress of Black Women, the National Association of Female Executives and Women in Public Policy among others.

Considering herself to be a world traveler, Mrs. Brown's most recent ventures include an excursion to the People's Republic of China and a journey to the country of South Africa. Mrs. Brown currently resides in the suburbs of Maryland with her husband of 25 years, who is a local attorney. She is also the mother of two college-aged sons.

Contact:
Anise Key Brown
P.O. Box 524
Brookeville, Maryland 20833
(301) 682-6494
anise1@verizon.net

SEVENTEEN

LEARNING TO TRUST AGAIN

By Anise Key Brown

Have you ever felt the pain of being deceived or betrayed, and lost your trust in someone? I know the pain was riveting, and you probably just wanted to close the book on that chapter of your life. Let's just cut to the chase. Trust is one of those emotionally charged words that run the gamut on the emotional scale. It can elicit a paradox of feelings from fear and love, to faith and betrayal. If trust were a commodity on the stock market, it would be invaluable. However, it is something that cannot be sold, bought or traded. Trust is innate and must come from within. In the Washington, D.C. region where I live, trust is indeed a hot commodity. In a political world of intrigue, intelligence and espionage, the issue of trust can indeed become a difficult word and has placed many a person in a challenging situation. I once ran a campaign where the slogan was, "Who do you trust?" In this instance, it was partisan politics that asked the question of the voters, with an implication that the current office holders could not be trusted. They had failed to deliver on the promises to the people and the candidate was making a new offer. "Trust me" was the offer. "Give me a chance" was the new threshold. In other words, the candidate was asking the voters to trust again for what had been a previous failure. However, in the context of this chapter and topic, we are not referring to the political, legal, or scientific definitions of trust, but will limit our discussion to the sociological and more relevant psychological definition of trust. And that's when trust takes on a whole different persona. That's when the practice and not the theory of trust cuts through the very pit of our soul, our being, and who we are.

Once you have been betrayed, cheated on, lied to, stolen from, scammed, and bamboozled (among other unattractive and descriptive adjectives), it's hard, so very hard, to go back and trust again. Very hard, indeed! The breakdown of trust creates pain, frustration, disillusionment, depression, repression, guilt, anger, loneliness, heartache, bitterness, and a whole host of ugly words and demoralizing feelings. First of all, how do we define trust, and secondly, how do we give it a second chance or another try? What does it take to forgive, forget, and learn to trust again? What does "again" mean? One thing is clear; we certainly cannot go through life without ever being able to trust anyone else again, when another has hurt us. We go through life trusting things without a second thought. It's a part of our daily ritual. We trust that our car will start, the signal light will change as programmed, our remote control will mute the television commercial that we do not want to hear for the umpteenth time, and that our microwave oven will function on command. When these things fail us, however, we take our car to the mechanic, we change the battery in the remote control, and we revert back to Driver's Ed 101 and remember the four-stop approach to get through the intersection.

These are all very basic thoughts and feelings about everyday functions regarding the word trust. We don't give these things a second thought as we maneuver through everyday life. In other words, we put these minor annoyances in perspective and keep right on living. But trust in and of itself can be as simple, and yet as complex as the intense feelings that it provokes.

The definition of trust is indeed an emotional and passionate debate. In almost every society, it is one of those virtues that we hold in the very highest of esteem. Regardless of which definition you may use, Webster, Merriam or Wikipedia, the word conjures intense feelings, particularly if you have been violated, betrayed, almost destroyed, or broken in any way. So what does **trust** mean? Basically, trust is defined as assured reliance on the character, ability, and strength of someone or something. It is defined as that in which confidence is placed; a strong belief that some person is honest or can de depended upon; a strong sense of reliance conveyed to an individual or thing; the condition and resulting obligation of having absolute certainty in the trustworthiness of another. The word trust connotes words such as faith, dependence, care, conviction, belief, integrity, confidence, reliance, loyalty, honesty, and other serotonin-based descriptions. Trust also means to place something in the care of. A trustworthy person is someone we can place our trust, and rest assured that the trust will not be betrayed, destroyed or broken.

So what does the word **again** mean? Again means once more, a repeat or return, anew; to return to a previous place, position or state. So what does Learning to Trust Again really mean?

Trust is a key component in our lives. It's the most delicate yet powerful thing that dictates a human being's psyche. It's what the world thrives on. It is how families and relationships grow stronger, and it gives you the protected feeling when you know you can trust someone or something that is important to you in life. You never quite realize how important trust is until it's no longer there, and you must learn to trust again.

There are many levels of trust to be dealt with throughout life in which you'll have to gauge and predict if there's any way to trust in the future. Though you may not trust a particular situation or person because the trust barrier has been broken, you must not allow those situations to dictate how you trust again in the future. An important rule of the road to learning to trust again is forgiveness. In the process of forgiveness, we have to let go of the past. As you realize that your past does not determine the outcome of your future, you can release the hurt and pain.

In order to go through life as peaceful as possible, and for the restoration of your own soul, you have to learn to trust again. There are many valid reasons to learn to trust again. First, trust restored may not be with the same person, group or community, but you must learn to trust again to save your own soul. You cannot continue to cling to the past. You may ask yourself, "How foolish would I be to allow myself to fall into that same trap again?" But the real question is, how foolish would you be if you never allowed yourself to trust again, and live a life without the optimism and positive attributes that accompany a life of trust. The bitterness of looking at everyone with a jaundiced eye, suspicion and question will constantly present an unhappy and uncomfortable place in your soul and in your spirit. Most relationships are vital to our well-being and require some level of trust in order for us to live effectively. Another reason is because everyone deserves a second chance; the person who harmed you may have really changed, or may really have a desire to change. This individual may feel awful that they have hurt you. But they really do love you, and want to repent for their mistakes and the pain that they caused you. There are, however, certain steps and commitments that must be taken in order to prove the restoration of your trust in them. Getting counseling and dealing forthrightly with all of the symptoms and ramifications that may have been contributing in the violation of trust is a must. And lastly, you must learn to trust again to give someone else or someone new a first chance. You don't want to forever blame someone else for some harm that another person has caused you, particularly when they did not have anything to do with the infraction or transgression in the first place, and was not where in site when you lost your trust in the perpetrator. The doors of trust should not be shut on what could possibly be one of the best relationships in your life, whether personal or professional.

There are different levels of trust that we encounter everyday. These are everyday trust, the trust of competence, which is also referred to as licensed trust, and the more intense trust of intimacy. Everyday trust is getting up in the morning and turning on a hot shower, or knowing there will be a floor beneath your feet when you get out of bed. The trust of competence includes such things as hiring a plumber and assuming that he can fix the leaky faucet, or picking up a newspaper and trusting that the reporter has gotten the facts in the reporting of an accurate article. The CNN cable news network markets that it is the most trusted name in news. You expect the brakes on your car to function properly after your mechanic has repaired your vehicle. Society contributes to the trust of competence by requiring certain fields to be licensed, barred or certified. These requirements increase our trust in the people that are performing these tasks for us, and that they know what they are doing. However, there are times when this type of trust has been compromised. You ask your hairdresser or barber to trim just a little hair and that you will not get up from the chair balder than you had intended. Many a relationship like this has been damaged, and the victim has never returned to sit in that chair again. However, this final level of trust is the one that makes us most vulnerable, for there are no licenses or certifications or exams to render them trustworthy, only our deep and abiding faith that the person will be honest, reliable, and to whom we can place our confidence. It is the violation of this level of trust that can send us riveting into emotional stakes that take years to heal, and oftentimes not at all.

As stated earlier, this kind of trust is innate and must be rendered from within. These are the degrees of trusted relationships, where the self is made vulnerable and the trust takes on a higher level of expectation and commitment, including vows such as those recited in a marriage. You confided something personal to a friend and trusted that they would not share your personal information with the chatty office gossip. This kind of trust may be with a business partner who, without your permission, borrows an enormous amount of money for personal use, such as to pay cash for a new car for his mistress. You trust your boss to give you the raise that he promised, after you successfully completed the project. It could be a son or daughter for whom you are paying college costs, only to find out the week before the planned graduation that your child flunked out more than a year ago. You ask how could this happen? Ask any parent who has experienced the heart wrenching pain and devastation, and you will recognize how this disregard for trust can significantly alter the relationship.

Eventually, everyone must have their own individual measuring tool for when and how they will ever trust again. Some people require higher standards before they can ever learn to trust again. More hoops must be jumped through, more rivers swam, more mountains climbed.

One of the most tormenting and devastating kinds of abuse of trust is that which happens in a marriage. In this instance, vows have been broken, and too often irreparable harm has been done. Scott Haltzman, psychiatrist and author of "The Secrets of Happily Married Men", says, "A spouse who has been a victim of a cheating partner should require more than a simple "forgive me". My twenty-one year old son (who has yet a lot of living, learning, and loving to do), says that trust for him is one of the most important factors in his future relationships. He dated his former girlfriend all four years of high school, and everyone just knew it was going to be one those "I married my high school sweetheart" love stories. However, during their senior year, she placed a hot kiss on the lips of another young man at a party. He has yet to forgive her. They broke up, and even though she has continued to pursue a second chance for the last four years, he vehemently attests that his trust in her has been permanently shattered.

There is no trusting again in this instance. He was in a situation where he was in relationship during high school for all four years with a girl that lived in the neighborhood. Throughout high school, everything was fine, everyone thought that they were going to be together for a long time, and that they were the perfect match. His biggest issue in the relationship was trust. He thought he would always be able to trust her, until she cheated on him, and he found out through another source going to class one day. He states that he had to keep everything in perspective when the terrible news dawned on him. His first question was, could he ever trust this person again, and secondly, how would this affect his future in similar situations dealing with the same issue. For him, he knew he could never trust her again, and had to have enough respect and love for himself not to let this just pass up and move on. He called her the same night and they broke up, letting her know that his trust for her was gone, and that he couldn't trust her again in similar situations.

That was years ago, and to this day she still tries to get back together, not knowing there's no chance, simply because the trust could never be there again. He understood that, just because the situation did not work out due to trust, he couldn't allow his future trust to falter because he was holding on to one situation. And yet, we can all recall more troubling relationships where the husband slept with the wife's best friend, or the teenage daughter is pregnant by the live-in boyfriend.

Learning to trust again is a painful process, but what is ultimately more painful is the carrying around, for the rest our lives, excess baggage. It only weighs us down ad takes away our joy. So, how do we begin to navigate the winding and treacherous road back to trust? When learning to trust again, you must categorize everything that has happened in that situation, weigh your pros and cons, and ask yourself, "Is it really worth it?" The common mistake people make in trusting again is they overlook the value in trust, and don't take the time to realize how critical it is in making things work in life. In learning to trust again, you must have the ability to wipe the slate and the past clean, and have the confidence to start fresh in your newfound situation, always letting yourself know that trust is critical from start to finish. The next time you are faced with a situation where trust is lost or trust needs to be regained, make a list of all the things major in your life you trust and why. Once you have done that, make sure you are demanding the same thing and getting the same from whoever or whatever you are trying to trust again. Let your decision of how to handle trust be gauged by your own personal references, and things that are already making you happy in life, simply because we trust them.

Exercise

So, as we get behind the wheel and adjust the rearview mirror, we need to ask ourselves seven hard "heart" questions before we start the ignition.

1) Without becoming a victim to the act of betrayal, what questions do you need to ask yourself? Did you "trust" too much? Were there warning signs of early little white lies, half-truths, and other factors, that you did not want to consider? Were you in denial? Were you afraid of confrontation? Did you just hope that the honest gut wrenching feelings of antennas swirling in your stomach and head would just go away? This is a good time for us to examine ourselves, and our own standards of what kind of relationship we really want. Broken trust in relationships provides us with the fortitude to make progress in building up our self-esteem and self-trust. We utilize a degree of discernment in determining what has personal credibility for us. Good self-examination and reflection are the first steps toward rebuilding and learning to trust . Start with believing in yourself again. You are most important. Don't fail yourself.

2) Has this person or act of transgression hurt me so deeply that I would prefer to move on? If I decide to move on, will there be second thoughts? This is a very important question, and only you can determine if a person warrants another chance to be trusted. If your best friend slept with your husband while you were away visiting your sick mother, then you may have to decide if either of these people (husband or best friend) deserves to still be a part of your life.

3) Do I truly believe that this person is really sorry for this wrong, and is the individual willing to take ALL the steps necessary to right this wrong? If this is the case, am I truly willing to forgive and forget?

4) If I am <u>not</u> willing to separate from the person permanently, as in moving on, am I willing to negotiate a set of conditions that I can truly live with for a very long time?

5)   How long has this act of betrayal been a part of my everyday existence? How long have I been living with this act of transgression? Three months, six months, one year or more? Am I constantly reliving and feeling the pain on a daily basis? Has it become a part of my psyche? My state of mind?

6)   What advice would I give to my daughter, my best friend, or another sister, who is going through the same emotions?

7)   Do I need professional help at this point in my life, in order for me to live again?

One thing that you can trust is that life is always changing. Relationships will evolve, resolve, and dissolve, and in each of these transformations, you will have to accept what is, with a commitment to maintain a strong sense of well-being. You may have trouble trusting new situations, but you cannot give up. The process will be difficult, but it will be worth it. So go ahead, take the wheel, start the ignition, and even if you have to accelerate slowly on the back road of trusting again, move forward, one block at a time. You know the saying, "Time heals all wounds." Trust. Again. You will not only survive, but also thrive. And drive. Go ahead. It's your life. It's time to live and love, and yes, trust again!

Recommend Readings

The Courage to Trust: A Guide to Building Deep and Lasting Relationships, Cynthia A. Wall and Sue Thoele.

Ask Barbara-100 Questions on Love, Sex and Relationships, Dr. Barbara D'Angeles.

When Your Lover is a Liar: Healing the Wounds of Deception and Betrayal, Susan Forward.

Too Good to Leave, Too Bad to Stay, A Step-by-Step Guide, Mira Kirshenbaum.

After the Affair: Healing the Pain and Rebuilding Trust When a Partner Has Been Unfaithful, Janis A. Spring.

ABOUT THE AUTHOR

SONJA SENHOUSE WILSON (SSW)

Sonja Senhouse Wilson is President and CEO of Break Through Development Group (BTDG), an organization that seeks to empower women emotionally, spiritually and physically by discussing and addressing issues that affect women in their personal and professional daily lives.

For the past three years BTDG has been charged with the mission to free women from low self image and improve heighten self respect. BTDG has achieved this by speaking, teaching and training in the areas of self esteem, prayer life and self image. BTDG has been invited to speak in New York, New Jersey, Connecticut and Oklahoma on issues affecting women.

SSW was born in Trinidad, West Indies and raised in the United States. She is a graduate of College of Mt. Saint Vincent where she received a dual Bachelor of Arts degree in Sociology/Communications Arts while she trained in Social Work. Social Work is where she developed an understanding of and a love for women of all cultures. She is a candidate for her MBA in marketing at Wagner College. SSW has traveled the world as a professional model and has graced the pages of Vogue, Cosmopolitan, Seventeen, and Essence and Ebony magazines. She has also been featured in many ad campaigns such as L'Oreal Cosmetics and Avon.

SSW is a member of The Professional Woman Network (PWN). SSW holds membership in other professional organizations such as National Professional Executive Woman (NAFE). She is active within her church and community and serves as a role model for children and youth.

Contact:
Break Through Development Group
P.O. Box 9306
Elizabeth, New Jersey 07202
(908) 294-2465
SonjaWilson3@aim.com

EIGHTEEN

FORGIVING YOURSELF AND OTHERS

By Sonja Wilson

What is forgiveness and why forgive? Have you ever held onto a grudge or emotions of mistrust, hurt and anger inside that you know are tearing you apart? We cannot deny that at some point in our lives we have held onto hurt feelings that have plagued our minds. It is only until we forgive ourselves and others that we can live in total freedom and victory. Forgiveness is not what we feel and is not the same as trust. To forgive doesn't mean that you will forget what was said and done to you. Forgiveness is the ability to stop allowing others to control your life by their offenses towards you.

Imagine a young girl at the age of thirteen being called "you little whore" repeatedly by her mother. Sarah was bright, energetic and fun-loving. She loved life and dreamed of being a famous actress. Her self-esteem and dreams were crushed when, at the tender age of thirteen, her mother screamed at her to "get out of my house and don't come back!" Why? Was it because Sarah showed an interest in Jeff, the varsity basketball player at her local high school? Was it the pressures of her mother raising her child as a single parent, or was it selfishness that prompted Sarah's mother to behave offensively? Sarah vividly recalls having reoccurring nightmares of the slamming door that closed behind her on that cold winter night. Her eyes filled with tears, her body shaken and her thoughts confused, she walked aimlessly seeking a sign as to what she would do. She walked five miles to her grandmother's house. Sarah hated what her mother had said to her, and even though her grandmother tried to comfort her, she couldn't erase the deep-seated pain that she had endured. Sarah was controlled by destructive thoughts and feelings that ruled her life. She felt dirty, unworthy, unloved and unaccepted. How could she ever feel dignity again? Aren't self-respect, self-worth and self-dignity birthrights?

Nothing can be more painful than having indignity dumped upon you. No purpose is served when you allow people and their wrongdoings to deter you from your dreams. It is understandable that, when your self-worth and dignity are undermined, resentment may fester. Yet, no matter how much the resentment is justified, it is still more self-destructive to the person harboring the anger than to the other person. The resentment can also cause blockage to your personal and professional development.

Sarah lived with un-forgiveness for most of her adult life. It was seventeen years later, at the age of thirty, that Sarah unleashed the chains of un-forgiveness that had bound her. Sarah truly forgave herself, and then her mother. It was excruciating to go back in time and dredge up painful memories of feeling rejected and emotional abandonment. Sarah recounted numerous times that her mother belittled her. The process was agonizing. Sarah suffered guilt, shame, blame and anger. Her thoughts were self-destructive as she constantly contemplated what she did wrong and why she wasn't good enough.

Sarah sought understanding from praying and reading self-help books. She realized that her resentment and deep-seated anger was towards her mother crippling her in all areas of her life, especially love relationships. Sarah didn't understand that she was carrying a heavy emotional baggage that interfered with her relationship with her husband, her two children, and even the team of workers she supervised. Sarah became suspicious about other people's motives, behaviors and attitudes, when in fact they were accepting and loving toward her. Sarah would have outbursts of anger, not realizing it was because of her unresolved shame and guilt from her mother's offenses. Sarah chose to forgive herself and her mother. She was convinced if she didn't offer forgiveness she would never live a quality life. Sarah realized that her ability to love her mother was tied directly to her ability to forgive her for all of her insensitivities. Sarah had to release the guilt, shame and blame about what she experienced as a young girl.

Learn a lesson from Sarah. Don't hold onto un-forgiveness for years because of a wrong that you have suffered. The failure to forgive stems from the lack of desire to forgive. But we all have the *ability* to forgive. When we fail to forgive, we can go for years and years unknowingly corrupting ourselves and sabotaging our own happiness. When we find it difficult to love someone who has wronged us, it is often linked to the refusal of forgiving that person. It doesn't matter who the perpetrator was. You may say, "What does forgiveness have to do with my pain?" "Why should I forgive my mother? She ruined my dreams!" "Why should I forgive my father? I never knew him!" "Why should I forgive my parents? After all, they divorced each other!" "Why should I forgive my friends for gossiping about me? They violated my trust!" "Why should I forgive my spouse for cheating on me? I was so in love!" Take control by committing to be emotionally free from un-forgiveness so that you may enjoy the rest of your life. Start by forgiving yourself, an essential choice to your future successes.

Forgiveness revolves around two internal processes:

1. Self Forgiveness: releasing of guilt and shame.

2. Forgiveness of others: necessary for building strong healthy relationships.

Exercise
FORGIVING YOURSELF—The choice is yours.
To increase the ability to forgive yourself, answer the following questions. Be detailed.

• What hurtful experiences are you holding against yourself that you need to release and forgive?

_____

_____

• How can you forgive yourself for being the one who broke the trust?

_____

_____

• How can you forgive yourself for violating another human being?

_____

_____

- How can you forgive yourself for victimizing others?

_____

_____

- Can you forgive yourself for being too weak?

_____

_____

- Can you forgive yourself for being too imperfect?

_____

_____

Seven Practical Steps to Self-Forgiveness

1. Accept that you have faults and make mistakes; accept who you are.

2. Let go of resentment, self-anger, self-hostility, and self-destructive behaviors for failures.

3. Love yourself and embrace self-love after you have acknowledged your failure.

4. Let go of the need to overcompensate for past misdeeds and reject the burden of guilt.

5. Don't suffer regret over a self-inflicted grievous personal offense.

6. Develop a personal spirituality to allow healing of your heart.

7. Think happy thoughts and trust in yourself.

FORGIVING OTHERS—The key to your inner healing.

To increase the ability to forgive others, answer the following questions honestly:

• Who are the people in your life that you feel have mistreated you?

_____

_____

• Why should you forgive the offender? Shouldn't the offender be punished?

_____

_____

• Why does the offender deserve your forgiveness?

_____

_____

• Is it in your best interest to forgive? Why?

_____

_____

Eight Practical Steps to Forgiving Others

• Identify and replace wrong beliefs that block your ability to forgive others.

• Know that you are able to forgive others.

• Realize that anger does not feel good.

• Recognize that un-forgiveness comes from hurt feelings, not what actually offended you.

- Don't allow another person's actions and words to cause you anger and pain.

- Don't try to control another person's actions.

- Be honest regarding hurts, pains and offenses suffered.

- Let go of past hurt and pain.

Forgiveness takes time. Take time to heal.

HEALING PROCESS—Daily exercises.

Exercise

Self-Forgiveness Exercise: Every morning before you begin your day, look directly into the mirror and recite, "There is nothing to gain by holding myself in un-forgiveness, and there is everything to gain by releasing myself from un-forgiveness and starting the process of healing. I desire to move forward to make a positive difference in my future. I can and will forgive myself. I am fearfully and wonderfully made. I will no longer punish myself, and I will not be angry with myself for making mistakes. I choose to forgive myself. I forgive myself for allowing _____ (name whatever the hurt is) to control me, and for hurting others out of my hurt. I reject this behavior. I have a positive forgiving attitude, and I will no longer hold unto un-forgiveness of myself."

Remember, it takes time to walk in forgiveness. Be patient. Journal your feelings about this exercise for seven days and review your thoughts. Repeat when necessary.

Exercise

Forgiving Others Exercise: Identify people or circumstances that you feel have robbed you of your personal power. Your personal power is forfeited when you hold unto un-forgiveness. You can write a letter to each person who has wronged you. You simply have chosen not to allow another person's actions and words to cause you anger, hurt and resentment. You can either mail the letter, or keep it in a safe place. (See following example.)

Visualize the person who has wronged you standing in front of you as when they first committed the offense. Have an imaginary conversation with that person. Here is a model dialog, "It is foolish of me to pretend that you did not hurt me, when in fact you did. Perhaps it was unintentional, but when you said and did _____ (name offense), I was hurt and angry. Every time I think about what you said and did, I feel resentment, bitterness, anger and pain. I no longer choose to hold unto these negative thoughts. I realize that everyone, including myself, is absorbed by self-interest. Out of my own self-interest, I became annoyed by your expression of your self-interest. I would have preferred you did _____ or said _____, but you didn't. You are responsible for your own actions and I am responsible for mine. I no longer place the burden of my expectations on you. I forgive you and accept you for who you are."

Journal your feelings about this exercise.

BENEFITS OF FORGIVENESS—

The best antidote to un-forgiveness is a well-lived life. Benefits include:

• Moving from resentment and disharmony with others and within ourselves

• Moving towards harmony, trust, reconciliation and resolution

• Learning to love ourselves and others despite our failings

• Improved mental and physical health

- Increased courage and strength

- An appreciation for the beauty and goodness that surrounds you

- Awareness of peace

CONSEQUENCES OF UN-FORGIVENESS—
   A negative legacy

- Loss of love for self and others

- Overwhelmed by fear of rejection

- Low self-esteem and low self-worth

- Unresolved hurt, pain and suffering

- Living in an emotional vacuum, little or no emotions are shown and shared

- Emotional and physical illness caused by anger, criticism and resentment

- Constantly replaying hurt and seeking revenge (wasted energy)

FORGING AHEAD—
   Let go and live in freedom. You will have:

- Freedom to forgive

- Freedom to love

- Freedom to live

- Freedom to grow

To forgive is the most powerful weapon in your possession. Use it in the battle of life in order to win the war. Don't let un-forgiveness hold you captive any longer. When we forgive ourselves and others, we must go through an initial grief. We first must acknowledge that we have been hurt, in order to let go of all our past hurts, so we can press forward. We cannot undo the events of the past, but we can do something about our present future. The choice to forgive yourself and others is one of the best decisions you will ever make for your life journey. You can change the direction of your life by actively walking in forgiveness. Choose to forgive today. You will make yourself and others happy. Just imagine yourself being freed from an enormous burden that was placed on your shoulders, causing you to walk in a stooped manner, looking down instead of onward and upward. You are freed from the burden that caused your mind to second guess your decisions based on your emotional baggage. Now visualize yourself unburdened by all that excess weight. See yourself walking erect, looking ahead to a bright and promising future.

PROMISE OF COMMITMENT—
Endless possibilities are gained when you forgive.

Exercise
On _____, I _____, have gained a better understanding of forgiving myself and others. I am committed to forgive myself and others from my heart to allow healing and peace to flow into my life.

Recommended Readings

Forgive for Good by Frederic Luskin, Ph.D.

www.learningtoforgive.com

www.coping.org

www.forgivenessday.org

ABOUT THE AUTHOR

SELERIA JEAN WILLIAMS

Seleria Jean Williams is a licensed and certified speech-language pathologist in Pennsylvania and Delaware. She is Founder, President, and CEO of The Total Woman Institute for Career and Personal Development, offering professional and personal development training, self-esteem and leadership development training, life style coaching, and professional consulting services for women. Seleria is a certified by The Professional Woman Network (PWN) as a Diversity Trainer with special emphasis in women's issues, diversity, and multiculturalism. She has been recently appointed to serve as a member of the International Board of Directors of The Professional Woman Network (PWN). Seleria is also a member of the Professional Woman Speakers Bureau.

As an independent contractor of speech-language services, she specializes in the treatment and management of neurogenic speech and language disorders, management of dysphagia and other swallowing related disorders, voice and diction improvement, accent reduction, and communication skills development. With over 28 years of experience in her profession, she is passionate about the health and well-being of today's woman with a special interest in empowering women to achieve optimal physical, emotional, and spiritual health. In addition to her experience as a Speech-Language Pathologist, Seleria serves as a mentor for children with special needs and serves on the Board of Trustees for Special Olympics for Philadelphia.

Seleria holds a Bachelor's degree in Speech Pathology and Audiology from Southern University A & M College in Baton Rouge, Louisiana and a Master's degree in Speech-Language Pathology from Louisiana State University. Her employment history includes experiences in public schools as a resource teacher, public school Speech-Language Pathologist; Clinical Rehabilitation Director various outpatient and sub-acute healthcare facilities; Clinical Coordinator and Classroom Instructor for the Speech-Language and Hearing Training Program at Tennessee State University; guest lecturer in the Human Behavioral Services certification program at Washburn University in Topeka, KS; and adjunct faculty member at West Chester University in West Chester, PA. Seleria holds membership in the American Speech-Language and Hearing Association, Delta Sigma Theta Sorority, Inc, Chester County Chapter of the Drifters, Inc., and at her church she is active in various church ministries, including the Mind, Body and Soul Ministry. Seleria serves as a role model for women and youth in the different organizations of which she holds membership. She currently resides in West Chester, PA., and has two daughters, Mignon Cyrelle and Aria Nicole Williams. Seleria is available for workshops, public speaking events, and consulting projects.

Contact:
The Total Woman Institute for Professional and Career Develpoment
Seleria Jean Williams
P. O. Box 1732
West Chester, PA 19380-0058
(484) 252-6200
Email Address: sjw1916@yahoo.com

NINETEEN

PERSONAL PRESENTATION STYLE: LETTING YOUR VOICE BE HEARD

By Seleria Williams

I can remember as a child, the first time in my life when I was asked to take the lead role in a church Christmas program. I felt truly honored, special, and quite privileged to have been selected to have a major role in the Christmas play, yet I was extremely anxious and nervous about taking on this challenge. Challenged because I had to memorize my speaking parts for a three-act play, and frightened because this performance would take place in front of a live audience of familiar and unfamiliar faces. Being the shy and soft-spoken person that I was,

I feared that I would stammer through my speaking parts, forget my lines, forget my cues, my prompts, and look like a total idiot. I wanted so badly *not* to participate in the Christmas program, but I knew that it would have been a big disappointment to my family, friends, and Sunday school teachers if I turned down the role. I couldn't disappoint these people because they were always there for me, encouraging me, grooming me, and preparing me for life's greatest moments. They wanted me to experience a shining moment in my life and this opportunity seemed to have been that moment.

With lots of encouragement from my family, church members, and the Christmas program facilitator, I found the courage to stand up to that challenge, and I acted out my parts with much success. This was accomplished through extra practice drills at home and oral reading assignments during class time from my grade school teacher. I familiarized myself with the entire Christmas skit, performed mock rehearsals of my part only in my own home in front of the mirror in my bedroom. There were extra rehearsals and tough-love discussions with a favorite 4th grade teacher, family members, and my Sunday schools friends. My determination and quest to be a "star performer" in the Christmas program allowed me to be successful. I knew what had to be done and knew that if I practiced and prepared myself well in advance, I could handle the speaking parts and act out my role with confidence. I continue to find this concept to be true even today in my adult life, where the multiplicity of tasks and demands of my time are now far greater than my childhood responsibilities.

We can all become influential speakers and master the art of public speaking if we learn to engage in early preparation and pre-planning of the details required of us.

The art of public speaking and oral presentations is dependent upon how prepared we are to utilize our voice and creative minds to make our messages meaningful and persuasive enough to command the attention of our audiences. Our speech is that one mechanism by which we can express our thoughts, feelings, and impart critical information to others. It is so important that our speech is intelligible and understood by our listeners. How we produce specific sounds in words can enhance the listeners learning style, or result in confusion and lack of comprehension.

Now let's take a peek at how our speech imparts knowledge and understanding:

- **Vocal Quality:** perceptual aspect of a speaker (whiney, raspy, whispery, harsh, hoarse, hard/soft voice)

- **Pitch:** listener's perception of spoken words ranging from the highness or lowness of a sound

- **Intensity:** force or stress by which a sound is produced by a speaker; loudness

- **Articulation:** the means by which speech sounds are formed and shaped by the speech organs (i.e., lips, tongue, jaw, teeth, etc)

- **Respiration:** the act of breathing; the energy source for speech. There are two cycles of respiration, inhalation and exhalation.

- **Resonation:** a quality given to sound to describe the richness and variety of sound

- **Intelligibility:** a degree of clarity by which one's speech is understood by a listener, which is greatly impacted by articulation, rate, vocal quality, fluency, and intensity

- **Intonation:** the rise and fall in pitch of the voice in speech

- **Rate:** speed by which speech sounds and spoken words are produced; a speaker's speech sound flow

- **Rhythm:** movement or tempo of the pattern of speech flow which is influenced by pitch, loudness, and quality (i.e., "choppy speech" vs "smooth speech)

- **Fluency:** smoothness by which speech sounds, syllables, words, and phrases, are joined together resulting in clear speech

Have you given much thought to how your speech and style of delivery is perceived by your listener? Let's first start with a quick assessment of your voice and the overall speech characteristics.

Exercise

Locate a tape recorder (one with good sound definition) and a 30-minute cassette tape. Record a 15-20 minutes sample of your normal speaking voice by reading a short passage from a magazine or a book, reading at your usual speed and rate, and using your everyday voice. Once you've recorded your voice, replay the tape and critique your voice. Rate your vocal parameters using a scale from 1-10 (1 being the lowest score and 10 being the highest) to assess the following characteristics:

Vocal Quality	1	2	3	4	5	6	7	8	9	10
Pitch	1	2	3	4	5	6	7	8	9	10
Intensity	1	2	3	4	5	6	7	8	9	10
Articulation	1	2	3	4	5	6	7	8	9	10
Respiration	1	2	3	4	5	6	7	8	9	10
Resonation	1	2	3	4	5	6	7	8	9	10
Intelligibility	1	2	3	4	5	6	7	8	9	10
Intonation	1	2	3	4	5	6	7	8	9	10
Rate	1	2	3	4	5	6	7	8	9	10
Rhythm	1	2	3	4	5	6	7	8	9	10
Fluency	1	2	3	4	5	6	7	8	9	10

Results

How did you rate? What vocal characteristics received a score of 8 and above? What vocal characteristics received a score of 5-7? What vocal characteristics received a score of 4 and below? Are you satisfied with the results? Is your voice loud enough? Did your voice project? Are you too soft spoken? Are there any words that you are having difficulty pronouncing? Is your speech fluent and intelligible? Do you feel that there is room for improvement? What two vocal characteristics do you consider to be primary targets for improving your speech or voice? What did you like and dislike about your voice? Are there vocal characteristics that are habitual that you feel cannot be perfected? Do you think professional help or training would be an asset to you, relative to improving your speech? Although this rating is not a scientific measurement of your vocal characteristics, it can serve as a generic indicator of your vocal output.

Exercise 2

Give the sampled recording of your voice to a friend or family member and have them critique your vocal parameters, using the same rating scale. Have them answer the same questions above and ask them to provide you with constructive feedback relative to your vocal characteristics, along with suggestions for improving your speech.

Effective Communication Style That Captures Understanding

In our quest for self-empowerment, we tend to seek opportunities where advanced skills and knowledge will position us for professional growth with increasing responsibilities and opportunities. We research and locate our professional publications for seminars, lectures, forums, and training classes based on our career objectives and personal goals. Course objectives, learner's expectations, and the skills to be mastered as a result of attending a class, lecture, or training series becomes increasingly important. This is particularly true if the course is a designed to be a self-help or motivational training piece. In deciding whether or not to attend a class or seminar, the topic and/or subject matter becomes critical and is given much consideration. We ask ourselves, "What's in it for me?" "What can I learn differently from what I already know if I attended this class/workshop?" "How can this training piece or the information presented improve my current situation or prepare me for a move to the next level in my career or personal life?" Some may also ask, "Who's the presenter?" or "Is this presenter a renowned educator/motivator?" and "Will he or she meet my expectations for presenting relevant information that's going to be beneficial to me?" This question typically tends to be the number one deciding factor that a participant considers before investing their money and time in pursing training seminars and workshops. In most instances, this is the one deciding factor, and therefore the person presenting the information for the course or training piece will need to verbally and mentally be prepared to provide the participants with a wealth of knowledge, skills, techniques, and strategies. **If that speaker so happens to be YOU, you will want to be prepared!**

Listed below are a few pointers and strategies to consider during the planning and preparation phase of your presentation. Remember, your presentation style reflects your personality and personal attributes.

1. Decide upon a subject or topic and outline your speech weeks or months prior to the presentation. Ask yourself, "If I were the participant, what kinds of information would I expect from the presenter?"

2. Build into your presentation essential components relative to the topic of discussion.

3. Write down ideas, quotations, and phrases that will add credibility to your presentation. You may want to draw or sketch images of how you will present the information to be covered. This may include pictures, graphs, charts, and slide presentations.

4. Obtain literature and other resources from the library, internet, professional publications, or from colleagues relative to your topic, and again make notes or highlight pertinent information that can be built into your presentation.

5. Research and seek the advice of experts or skilled professionals in your community or work place who can provide you with additional resources or visuals that can be incorporated into your presentation.

6. Research your audience and know whom you are speaking. If possible, obtain information regarding their professional and educational backgrounds, skill levels, and what they expect to obtain from your presentation. If you have an opportunity to speak with some of your potential participants prior to the scheduled presentation, find out what their expectations are and what they want to obtain from the training. Ask them how they plan to utilize the information. Try to target portions of your presentation to areas that have been identified as areas needing remedial training or areas lacking skill and precision.

7. Decide how you want to open your presentation – should you start with an ice-breaker to set the mood, a cartoon piece to enlighten the audience? Or should the day's presentation be introduced by telling a funny story about a recent experience you encountered moments prior to the start of the presentation. A relaxed and fully engaged audience from the start sets the tone for the entire presentation, especially for those participants whose behaviors and responses suggest that they have no interest in the day's event and would rather be someplace else doing something entirely different.

8. Decide how you want to end your presentation – should you recap the information presented through role-playing, group discussions, or audience interactions? Should you end the presentation with a question and answer session from the participants? Or, should you read a famous quote or selected poetry piece as a summary of the information that was presented? The closing remark and culminating activity will probably be the most remembered and most significant phase of the presentation.

9. Allow for opportunities to improve your speech, voice, and presentation style. Attend local workshops and seminars to observe and learn the techniques and delivery styles used by other presenters. We learn by seeing and doing, so seek opportunities to embrace growth.

10. Research your local community for organizations that may offer courses or speech clinics on developing public speaking skills (i.e., Toastmasters, Rotary Clubs). Many universities and colleges have Speech Language Pathology and Audiology programs that offer clinical services to the community for improving voice and diction, and accent reduction training. Many outpatient clinics offer similar treatment options. There are also licensed Speech-Language Pathologists who are trained to provide treatment strategies to individuals wishing to improve their communication skills (i.e., articulation, word pronunciation skills, voice and diction, accent reduction, etc.). Check with your libraries and community colleges to see if there are special courses offered during interim school sessions on public speaking or related topics.

11. Last and most importantly, practice your presentation weeks and days prior to the scheduled date. Again record and or/video tape your presentation and critique your delivery style. Write down your weaknesses and look for opportunities to correct those weaknesses prior to the actual presentation.

Exercise

According to Dale Carnegie, "It's Not Only What You Say, But How You Say It." He identified six common problems people have in speaking clearly: mumbling, speaking too fast, speaking too slowly, speaking in monotone, mispronouncing words, and using "filler" words such as "ya know", "okay", "uhhhh", or "yeah".

Question: What are your weak areas of speech?

1. _____

2. _____

3. _____

Just like when I was a little girl and was asked to take the lead in our church's Christmas play, the day may come when you are asked to stand before an audience. So that you are prepared, consider the following:

1. Expand your speaking vocabulary by utilizing words that reflect an intellectual style.

2. Obtain a dictionary and use it daily as a resource for developing your own vocabulary list, as well as opportunities to look up words that are unfamiliar to you, and to locate synonyms for words that may be appropriate for a specific concept.

3. Work on speech sound production as well as articulation by locating lists of words that are identified as "Words Most Often Mispronounced". Use a dictionary to identify correct pronunciation and diacritical markings to denote correct placement of stress in words.

4. Practice good articulation by making sure all sounds are produced correctly and ending sounds are produced and heard. Consider utilizing the expertise of a Speech-Language Pathologist if your speech requires professional training and remediation.

5. Tape your speeches and listen to determine whether your words are choppy or are crisp and clear. Is your rhythm and rate of delivery acceptable? Modify any flaw that you feel interferes with your ease of delivery.

6. When making an important point, pause before and after the idea. Allow for audience response and reactions.

7. Monitor you pitch so that your audience remains alert and involved in the presentation.

8. Make eye contact with your audience and remember the names of your participants so that, at given points during your presentation, you can add a personal touch by referencing a participant by name.

9. Speak with a loud strong voice and speak with conviction. Monitor your loudness level as needed. If a microphone is not available or not functioning, increase your voice and allow the audience to express their concerns with the level of your voice pitch loudness, rate, and delivery pace.

10. Always be prepared to take on new and different challenges as you build your skills and confidence in mastering public speaking and delivering oral presentations. Seek professional help if you lack skills and confidence.

11. Take a moment before and shortly after the presentation to pray and give thanks to God for the opportunities you've been given. Allow the spirit of his love and peace to transgress into your day. Stay positive and remain proactive even for those unexpected moments.

12. Believe in your self and other will too. Keep smiling and the world will smile back at you.

Final Exercise

List five (5) fears that you have regarding your personal communication and oral presentation skills:

1. _____
2. _____
3. _____
4. _____
5. _____

List five (5) things that you now can do to conquer those fears and increase your level of confidence:

1. _____
2. _____
3. _____
4. _____
5. _____

Remember the importance of the spoken word! Prepare yourself now to become an engaging and inspiring presenter of your thoughts and ideas. Public speaking can be a major fear for many, but if you are prepared, you will be truly successful when you deliver.

Recommended Reading

29 Leadership Secrets from Jack Welch by Robert Slater

Rich Minds, Rich Rewards by Valorie Raquel Burton

Public Speaking for Success by Dale Carnegie

Women of Faith – The Great Adventure: A Devotional Journey of the Heart, Soul, and Mind by Patsy Clairmont, Barbara Johnson, Marilyn Meberg, Luci Swindoll, Sheila Walsh, and Thelma Wells

Notes:

_____

_____

_____

_____

_____

_____

_____

_____

_____

_____

_____

_____

_____

_____

_____

_____

_____

_____

ABOUT THE AUTHOR

OCTAVIA SHAW

Octavia Shaw is President and CEO of the International Institute for Cultural Awareness (Washington, D.C), a cross-cultural consultant practice that focuses on micro and macro cultural dynamics in multiple settings (academic, vocational, workplace, religious facilities, family settings). She has traveled to several countries abroad and worked with clients in the U.S. to promote diversity and cross-cultural encounters.

Shaw received her bachelor's degree from Howard University in Journalism with a minor in Education. After assisting an ESOL (English for Speakers of Other Languages) teacher at a high school in Washington, D.C., her interest in the profession grew stronger and stronger. She worked for the Senate and then on the International Desk for a magazine company. She later joined the U.S. Peace Corps and served two years and West Africa in teaching English as a Foreign Language. Upon her return from Peace Corps, she was a Peaceworker Fellow at the University of Maryland Baltimore County. Shaw received her master's degree in Instructional Systems Development.

Shaw has been teaching, facilitating, training, and consulting for the past ten years and also continues to teach and coordinate in the field of adult ESOL and Literacy (for native and non-native English speakers).

Octavia Shaw is certified in diversity and women's issues by The Professional Woman Network and is involved in many community activities reaching out to others on these issues.

Contact:
Octavia Shaw
P.O. Box 31003
Washington, DC 20030
(202) 270-0646
E-mail: oshaw0405@yahoo.com
www.protrain.net

TWENTY

BREAKING THE SILENCE: CROSS-CULTURAL DIALOGUE

By Octavia Shaw

The world is not as you live it. We may want to think and believe that it is, but it really is not. The world is very intriguing because of the different people who inhabit the planet Earth. Our little daily world is just a microcosm of the world at large. There are many cultures and people with very different beliefs than yours. Let us take a journey now so that we may begin to break the barriers and silence, which are present when people do not understand one another.

What comes to mind when you think of "cross-cultural"? What comes to mind when you think of "dialogue"? "Dialogue" may be defined as conversation between two people. "Cross-Cultural" is an exchange between cultures.

The objective of this section is to determine if you're okay with being in a box regarding understanding other cultures, or if you are ready for help to get out of the box and encounter something that is unfamiliar to you.

Are You In the Box?

First of all, imagine yourself literally being enclosed and sealed in a box. How was that experience? If you're okay with it, then you can stop reading. If the experience was unpleasant and dissatisfying, then continue reading.

Secondly, imagine if everyone was exactly like you. Imagine everyone having your thoughts, feelings, ideas, mannerism, gender, religion, grew up where and how you grew up, had the same work ethics and style --- the same, the same, the same, the same. Whoa! How boring, unchallenging, mundane, and ridiculous is that? If we look at the possibility of learning about people different than we, then we may open our little world to a much larger universe that is filled with people just an unique as we are but different in their behaviors, traditions, appearance, and backgrounds.

Check all that applies

☐ I appreciate diversity and uniqueness.

☐ I don't go to the same restaurant all of the time.

☐ I communicate with others who don't speak the same language as I do.

☐ I spend time out of my neighborhood.

☐ I've traveled to another state.

☐ I've traveled to another country.

☐ I have friends of another race, ethnicity, gender, and/or religious background.

☐ I have friends outside of work.

☐ I don't mind if someone is "different" than I.

☐ I understand the values of others.

If you checked at least seven of these, you've stepped out of your 'world' and into that of someone else's. If you checked less than seven, then this is the opportunity for you to reach out and explore.

Encounter With Something That is Different

I must admit that encountering something different isn't easy. Once we become adults, we are often very set in our ways. It can be challenging to go a different route if you're not used to traveling multiple ways to and from various locations. Once we've mastered a language, it's difficult to learn another one in our adult stage. Research states that once a child is five or six, he/she has already learned his/her values. Children are not afraid to make mistakes. They are curious, interested, and grasp onto concepts pretty quickly. Adults are the opposite. However, we are not hopeless. We have the ability to continue to grow wiser. Therefore, to begin learning about new ideas and to broaden your mind (and step outside the box), consider these tips:

- Learn sign language, another spoken language, an instrument, and another field of study, profession, or sport.

- Learn to understand another religion other than your own.

- "Live in the shoes" of another gender or ethnicity.

- See what the city or a rural area is like for a day or a weekend.

Encounter/Exchange with Someone Who is Unique
You are indeed beautiful, unique, and special; others are too! Share something unique about yourself with another person and learn something unique about them.

List five things you would share that make you unique.
1. _____
2. _____
3. _____
4. _____
5. _____

List five things you would want to know about someone else that makes them unique:
1. _____
2. _____
3. _____
4. _____
5. _____

This is where the cross-cultural dialogue begins. How do you find someone with whom to have this dialogue? Is there someone that you were "dying" to talk to or find out about? Is there an ethnic group, race, or gender that you've wanted to find out about, but were afraid to ask? Is there someone with a different IQ, profession, or zip code that you've wanted to find out about? This is the opportunity. Reach out to the person and begin to exchange ideas, thoughts, and experiences. As Benjamin E. Mays said, "Nothing beats a failure, but a try." Once you've tried, you've aimed to succeed. When you don't have anything to aim for, there's no opportunity for growth and development. Reaching out to others shows interest. Interest shows our human nature of curiosity and heightens our awareness. Awareness enlightens and inspires! One reaches another. The encounter may develop a relationship or friendship. It may open doors to professional opportunities. It may strengthen our own personal development. It may make our inner circles stronger, more fulfilling and rewarding. It may positively influence political circles.

If you're afraid or would rather not dialogue with someone that you know or have been thinking about, here are some other ways to find someone.

- Join a club or an organization of interest.

- Take a class at the community college.

- Ask a relative, friend, neighbor, or co-worker.

- Travel out of town, state, or out of the country.

- Visit community cultural and ethnic fairs

- Visit a mosque, church, or synagogue.

My Experience in Korea

An encounter with a middle school student:

Female student: "Teacher, hair."
"Me":   "Yes, what about it?"
All other students: ooooooooooooooo

(It wasn't considered polite for the student to address something personal to the teacher such as asking about the texture of hair. However, they ALL were very curious.)

Me: (Laughed)
Students: (Started to laugh, too)
Female Student: "I want uhhhhh touch."

"I" thought that that one brave female student would come to touch my hair. I had braids. Before I could murmur 'yes' completely, they all ran to the front of the class to touch it. The other teachers thought that I had lost 'control' with the noise and 'wows'. They were also amazed that I allowed them to touch my hair. I didn't mind at all. This was a new experience for them. They had never touched an African-American's braided hair (with extensions) before. I continue to feel good about the decision I made about letting them satisfy their curiosity. They were simply curious.

My encounter with Koreans reminded me that in the United States, many people think that all Asians are the same. Koreans are different from Chinese. Chinese are different from Japanese. Koreans, Chinese, and Japanese people don't speak the same language. They don't have the same customs and belief systems. Speaking of stereotypes, I have learned that all Spanish-speaking people are not Mexican, nor are they all Latino. All Spanish-speaking people do not eat tacos and tortillas. And while we are talking about stereotypes, all African-Americans are not rappers, singers, actors/actresses, and dancers. All Africans didn't grow up in the bush. All Italians do not eat pasta. All Jews don't marry Jews. All men are not masculine. Everyone from the Caribbean doesn't eat jerk chicken, lie on the beach, or drink rum. These are stereotypes and generalizations. They are not always all true. They do not always apply to everyone of the same group.

Remember – you're getting out of the box; therefore, don't put anyone else in a box. It's about an exchange or an encounter of awareness. There are cultures within cultures. Therefore, the first encounter shouldn't have you judging the entire cultural community by just one person's behavior, appearance, or communication. Generally, one encounter may lead to another. Continue learning more about ALL people as it strengthens us, our families, our communities, and our society.

Exercise
1.   How do you identify yourself? (Caribbean-American, African, etc)

_____

2.   How do others identify you?

_____

3.   How do you want others to identify you?

_____

4.   How do you identify with _____ (choose any person, group, of a different background that yours):

_____

5.   How do they identify with you? (What do you have in common?)

_____

6.   What are your fears about

_____

7.   What do you perceive to be their fears about you?

_____

8.   How do you move beyond your fears?

_____

9.   How do you suggest they move beyond their fears?

_____

10. How do you appreciate each other?

_____

11. How do you try to understand one another?

_____

12. How do you embrace each other?

_____

13. How do you bring peace to each other?

_____

14. How do you befriend one another (if you choose to do so)?

_____

15. How do you share these cross-cultural encounters with your family (children, parents, siblings, etc.)?

16. How do you share these cross-cultural encounters with your community?

Involve your entire family in cross-cultural dialogues through:

- Exchange programs

- Focus Groups

- Seminars, workshops, and trainings

- Conferences

- Retreats

- Traveling

- Book Club meetings and discussion groups

Write an action plan and implement these strategies. Write down the task and give yourself a due date.

Avoiding Conflicts, Working Together, and Respecting Each Other: Cross Cultural Interactions

Keep in mind that when people of two very different cultures exchange ideas, there must be an awareness of differences. Keep the door open to dialogue and consider the following:

- Do not judge the other person.

- Be open-minded.

- Ask thoughtful and respectful questions about another person's culture.

    - What is the major religion?

    - What is the primary diet of most people?

    - When are meals served?

    - What type of music is most popular within the culture?

    - Describe the clothing.

    - What is the architectural style of the homes?

    - What are favorite cultural dances?

    - What are the most popular games for children?

    - What are hobbies that adults enjoy?

    - What happens to the elderly? Do they live in institutional homes for the aging or in family members homes?

    - What are the main goods that are manufactured in the country?

    - What crops are grown?

    - Is there gender equality?

There is so much that you can learn about others just by asking. But always be sure that you ask thoughtful, kind questions; the same kind of questions you ask of others, are the types of questions you may expect to be asked of you. The more respect we show others, the more respect we will receive in return.

The world would be a boring place if we were all the same. Reach out and embrace the differences between humans. God created each of us to be unique, and because we are to love one another, the best way to show this love is to reach out in kindness. May your journey to a greater acceptance of others be an exciting one.

ABOUT THE AUTHOR

STARLA PORTER

Starla Porter is president and founder of The Zoe Life Institute, a personal and professional development company. She has a strong desire to see all people live the life they were meant to live. She is equally passionate about the issues women face today, and believes that there is immeasurable power in the unity of strong and capable women.

Ms. Porter is a visionary, serving others for over twenty years. She has a Bachelor's degree in Business Management, and a Master's degree in Organizational Management. Upon receiving credentials by the State of California to teach business-related courses at both the high school and college levels, Ms. Porter chose to work as a substitute teacher and training workshop facilitator. Ms. Porter is also certified to train in Cultural Diversity, Women's Issue's, Women: A Journey to Wellness, Customer Service, and is a Certified Life Coach.

Ms. Porter is a keynote and motivational speaker. An advocate for mentoring others, she conducts a monthly support group, Sister Network, geared toward professional women.

Ms. Porter is excited about her future plans, which include establishing a Sister Network in every major city across the country. Her aim is to unite women from diverse backgrounds in an effort to establish friendships and connections, which under ordinary circumstances, these groups of women would never have had before.

Contact:
The Zoe Life Institute
P.O. Box 3671
Fontana, CA 92334
(951) 233-6076
thezoelife@aol.com
www.thezoelife.com
www.protrain.net

TWENTY-ONE

GO FOR IT! SETTING PERSONAL & PROFESSIONAL GOALS

By Starla Porter

Entrenched deeply within the African-American experience are two phrases that remind us, as women of color, the value of setting goals, whether they are personal or professional. These phrases have become so common that they echo within our souls and cause us to take notice when we extend ourselves in areas that don't support our reason for being.

"Write the vision and make it plain!"
"Without a vision the people perish!"

How many times have you heard these expressions only to make empty promises to yourself that "next time I'm going to write a vision for my life, or my career, and stick to it?" Don't answer that! I do however want you to consider the value of setting goals that will enable you to experience more frequent successes in your life, both personally and professionally.

What Are Goals?

Simply put, goals are something that you want to achieve and you are willing to expend time and energy towards its manifestation. A goal helps you aspire to something in the future and achieve more during your life. Individual goals will differ from woman to woman because they stem from your own interests and desires, not anyone else's.

Why Set Goals?

Generally speaking, women who set goals for themselves desire to live a more fulfilled and better life. These women want to be better people, have exciting professional careers, master a skill, or enhance their abilities. Whatever the reason, goals help you define what you want to accomplish in life. You set goals in different areas so you can evolve into a woman of substance who is results-oriented, and a better human being overall.

What is Goal-Setting?

Goal setting in its most simplistic definition is deciding what you want to do and making an action plan to do it. Once you have established a goal for yourself, you literally take steps towards its completion. You become committed and motivated to its realization.

Otherwise, it's easy to become distracted with day-to-day affairs and those areas which we value and esteem are neglected. Oftentimes, we never realize our life-long dreams, greatest ambitions or potential. As you discipline yourself to setting goals, you will discover you can and do have the power to control your fate in life.

> *"What you get by achieving your goals is not as important as what you become by achieving your goals."*
> — Zig Ziglar

Before you start the goal setting process, I want you to have all the tools necessary to see your goals through, starting with a goal setting theory that's focused on SMART goals.

What are S.M.A.R.T. Goals?

The source of SMART goals and its acronym have been lost over time, and there's a host of interpretations detailing what SMART goals actually stand for. However, despite the different interpretations, SMART goals still provide an excellent foundation for creating effective goals whether they are personal or professional. I will characterize S.M.A.R.T. in this fashion:

Specific

Measurable

Attainable

Realistic

Time

When you create your goals and remain true to this formula, it will help you stay focused upon what you ultimately want to achieve. The formula provides the structure to seeing your goals through.

Specific: A goal that is specific is well- defined, right to the point, and has a better chance of being accomplished than a nonspecific goal that's too broad and general. As you brainstorm your goals, consider the following:

(1) What do I want to achieve?

_____

(2) How much time should I allow?

_____

(3) What's the purpose or benefit of accomplishing this goal?

_____

(4) Does this goal require input from an outside source?

_____

(5) Are there any restrictions or conditions I need to meet prior to achieving this goal?

_____

Sisters, we can all agree that the "battle of the bulge" lingers near and far. Some of us lack the discipline to exercise, and we see the results 'growing' all around us. Couple that with rich, flavorful, creamy, hot, fried, mild and spicy foods of all types that are deeply rooted within our culture and the consensus would be — we like to eat!

A general goal would sound something like this: "I want to lose weight and get in shape." Here's an example of the same goal made specific that entails the five SMART points: "I will lose 25 pounds within 9 months. Doing so will cause me to be healthier physically, add years to my life, and boost my self-esteem. I will make some gradual changes in my diet by eliminating harmful foods that have been a part of my culture for generations. If my budget allows I will join a health club and commit to a program designed just for me. If not, I will not be deterred. I'll commit to walking 3-4 days a week and elevate to running as I feel stronger, making this routine a part of my life style. I will also invest in a good pair of athletic shoes and apparel to protect myself from the elements."

Another good example: "I'm going to save some money!" Clearly this is not specific enough, yet we proclaim this time after time without results. A specific goal involves you setting a desired amount that you want to save. Over what period of time do you want to have this money saved? Why are you saving the money? What's the purpose? Can you trust yourself not to dip into it or should you have someone hold it for you? And lastly, what personal sacrifices if any will you have to make to meet this goal? (Fewer spa trips or one less suit every month are decisions of sacrifice that you should be prepared to embrace. The results will be worth it!) By now you should clearly understand the value of setting goals that are specific, well defined, and to the point.

Measurable: A measurable goal means you will know when you have achieved it because you have established conditions for measuring your progress toward the success of each goal you set. You become more aware and informed of your progress, so it's easier to stay on point and focused on the desired results. Having set a very specific goal according to the guidelines provided will ensure your overall ability to measure your goals every time. How exciting your experiences will be as you begin to see results that will empower you to work even harder to achieving your goals! Sisters, keep this in mind. In order to know if your goal is measurable, you should be able to answer at least one (if not all) of the "how" questions: 1) How will I know if I have achieved my goal? 2) How many (dollars, pounds, etc)? 3) How much time will it take?

What better way to rate your progress than by utilizing a measuring system that's designed with your specific goals in mind! Let's consider one of the previously mentioned examples… "I will lose 25lbs within 9 months." This goal will be easy to track by periodically getting on the scale. The results don't lie. Either you have kept to the exercise routine or you have not. Either you have made changes in your eating habits or you have not. Or maybe you have been very diligent in one area and not the other. Understand this about setting and measuring a goal. Your measure of success, your measurability, depends totally upon every aspect of the specifics.

Attainable: My beloved sister, your goals should be something you have no doubt you will achieve, if you put your heart and soul into it! By identifying what's most important to you, you will no doubt develop an action plan for your success. Your overall attitude will intensify to the tenth power! You've heard these words before… "Faith without works is dead." If you don't set goals that you are willing to work hard for ⊠ it's just an empty dream. As you move forward and closer to the manifestation of your goals, you will discover sudden opportunities that you may have missed prior. These new discoveries will bring you even closer to your goals. They become attainable because your total mind-set is expanding with your goals; your self-awareness, self-image and self-esteem are soaring because you realize you deserve what you are striving for. Your goals should not only be specific and measurable, they should force you into action, because you know they are within your reach!

Realistic: This may sound a tad redundant, but to be realistic means you're willing to work for the goal you have set for yourself. Not only are you willing, but you are able to do this! If you can draw from past experiences, you may have noticed how projects that appeared to be the most difficult were easier to achieve than those on a smaller scale. I believe we garner greater motivation to tackle more demanding and complex projects; and so it will be with your goals. It becomes realistic to you when you believe whole-heartedly that you can make it happen. And if the target or goal is too low, you may not give it the attention it needs for you to succeed. There are a few other realistic components to consider: 1) Are you committed? 2) Do you have the time? 3) Know your limitations, and 4) Do you have the resources?

Resources can also be viewed as support. We often perform better when we know we have the support of others who believe in what we're capable of doing. Speaking of being capable, I have had a life-long dream of running in a marathon. Yet it would be unrealistic of me to register without any prior experience or serious preparation. So for now, it's a dream until I'm ready to make the decision to step out and commit for my success.

Time: The foundation of time says you have allotted sufficient time to achieve your desired results. You have established time limits that are not too short or too long to fulfill, and they are indeed reasonable.

As you initiate target dates for achievement, it will become necessary for you to devise a system or an approach that will allow you to keep up with your progress. Remember our "lose weight and get in shape" example? A tracking system for this goal could entail listing the starting weight alongside the desired weight; and on a bi-weekly basis notations could be made of the progress. Certainly there are many other ways to chart and time the overall progress; this is only one suggestion.

Another benefit of time is that it gives you a sense of urgency throughout the process up to completion. You consider all the phases and what needs to be done and when. Instead of just talking about it, you *become* it! Time makes you accountable to your goal. If goal setting becomes an intricate part of your success, make sure they are S.M.A.R.T. goals, for they will definitely increase your chances of experiencing greater levels of achievement!

Set your Goals, Make your Action Plans, and Live Your Dreams!

A State of Progression

Have you ever noticed how much time we put into planning our dream vacations, our weekends at the spa, or catching up with Sister Friends than planning our lives? Many women don't take the time necessary to set goals. They live their lives by chance, whereby they experience fewer victories than they deserve. My role in your life right now is to encourage you to *not* manage your life on luck and happenstance. On a daily and regular basis, your actions should be purposeful and intentionally focused on goals that will evolve as events and situations in your life are subject to change.

Where are you today? Where do you want to be tomorrow? Have you created an action plan to get there? My hope is that you absorb all the insight provided within the pages of this book. Get excited about setting goals, whether they are personal or professional, and let that excitement move you closer to your desired results as the thought of achievement penetrates your heart. Allow your list of goals to become your personal mantra, your daily dose of affirmations. Read them over and over — saturate your conscious mind with your goals until something is released in your soul! Why? Because you have they power within you to make it happen, and your very detailed goals will guide you closer to your destiny in life. But the choice is yours. Many of you are right on target and just need a boost of encouragement and direction. I encourage you to maintain a state of progression. Don't become stagnant, and most certainly get ready for the next level of purpose in your life. If by chance you have yet to embrace the goal setting idea, why not make a conscious decision to accept the challenge that's before you today? Who knows, you just might hit the mark!

Understand the state of progression as you consider your goals. Your desire to achieve more in life comes from within. Your inner witness for a more passionate and fulfilling life gives you the unction to function, the energy to forge ahead, the know-how to make something from nothing, and the wisdom to effectively move and operate within unfamiliar territory. The possibilities are endless, and opportunity awaits you every day, my Sister. It's time to start turning those dreams into goals, and then into reality. Those dreams that keep you awake in the wee hours of the night. You know, the thoughts that consume your every waking hour. You try to concentrate on someone else's need, yet your attention sways toward the vision in your heart. You try to give 100% on your job (bringing someone else's dream to life), but as time reveals itself, you become less and less enchanted about being there. You become disconnected, and you feel stuck like you can't get pass that point. I'm here to tell you that you can, and you are closer to fulfilling your goals than you know. Close your eyes and see what you believe!

Short or Long-Term Goals

No matter what objective or purpose you may have in setting goals, short or long-term, they both require you to make a first step. They both serve their purpose depending upon your desired outcome. Short-term goals are invaluable if your hope is to reach the finish line. Remember I shared my dream of running a marathon one day? That unquestionably is a long-term goal. I would be negligent in my preparation if I failed to establish a few short-term goals that will in due time get me to my long-term goal.

My short-term goals could involve me devising a tracking system where I would walk two minutes and run three minutes. Walk two, run three. Continue with this strategy until my endurance builds up. As my conditioning gets better, I can increase my intervals to five minute runs with a one-minute walk time in between. With dedication and commitment to the plan, my conditioning training will eventually pay off. I'll be better positioned to run a complete mile or two, increasing over time until I reach my ultimate goal. This example supports my long-term goal, yet not without identifying some short-term goals first.

A Lifelong Process

Your personal and professional goals will evolve over time, especially as you begin experiencing higher levels of achievement, as a result of setting goals for your life. The beauty of evolving over time is that your ambitions, your hopes and dreams, will evolve too. Your advancement and progression will empower you to establish and define new goals for yourself; you can expect your attitude and behavior toward setting goals to be an ongoing and consistent part of your life.

Remember our S.M.A.R.T. goals? Don't be afraid to create your own meaning to this goal-setting acronym. We identified S as Specific, but in addition to Specific it could mean Solid, Significant, and maybe even Stretch you into becoming the better person you strive to be. We explored M as Measurable, but how about Moving, Motivating, Meaningful and Memorable! Wow, the possibilities are endless. A was identified as Attainable, but consider Achievable or Action plans. R as Realistic can also be results-oriented or reasonable. And finally T for Time can mean Tangible or Thoughtful.

Whatever acronym you're drawn to, no one can rate your progress but you because you created your goals for yourself, by yourself. Even if you had some insight from another person, be it a mentor, coach, friend, or spouse. Ultimately the desired outcome is totally contingent upon you and falls solely upon your ability to make a plan and stick to it!

Let me be so bold to predict that the next time you hear these words bouncing through the airwaves, they won't find a place to land because you, my beloved Sister, have charted a new course; one that is fully and purposely controlled by you to your expectations! *"Write the vision and make it plain!"*… *"Without a vision the people perish!"* Setting personal and professional goals will become engrafted deep within your soul, and your expectations will soar. Commit to spending some quality time in prayer and meditating on your goals before you retire for the evening, and first thing in the morning. You will achieve greater and consistent successes because your vision in life will be clearly defined within the words of every goal you set for yourself; S.M.A.R.T. goals that are foundational to every level of achievement you will experience. Go for it my dear Sister, you deserve it!

My Short/Mid/Long Term Goals Defined

Short-Term Goals:

1. _____
2. _____
3. _____
4. _____
5. _____
6. _____

Mid-Term Goals:

1. _____
2. _____
3. _____
4. _____
5. _____
6. _____

Long-Term Goals:

1. _____
2. _____
3. _____

4. _____
5. _____
6. _____

ABOUT THE AUTHOR

SHARVA HAMPTON-CAMPBELL

Sharva Hampton-Campbell, a native of Louisiana, resides in Champaign, Illinois with her husband, Marshall, and her mother, Patricia. She received a Bachelor's and Master's degree in Social Work from the University of Illinois at Champaign-Urbana. Ms. Hampton-Campbell also completed paralegal training at Roosevelt University and conflict resolution and mediation training from Aurora University in Chicago, Illinois. She is employed full-time as an academic advisor at Parkland College and is an independent social work consultant and counselor. Currently, Ms. Hampton-Campbell is working on her clinical social work license.

Ms. Hampton-Campbell provides staff development training and workshops for public and private social service agencies, as well as youth seminars for churches, and community based youth organizations. She has developed and conducted the following workshops: "Becoming a Competent Case Manager," "It's all About the Attitude," "Engaging African-American Youth: A Strength's Perspective," and "Show Me the Money Financial Planning for Teens." She is also a Certified Trainer on women's issues, diversity and multiculturalism, and youth issues. Her latest projects are the development of Sista Circle, a Christian youth program that focuses on studying the word of God, giving back to the community and academic excellence, as well as Youth Empowered for Success (Y.E.S.), a therapeutic mentoring program for youth aged 11 to 18 years old.

Ms. Hampton-Campbell is a member of The Woman Professional Network International Advisory Board, and has received national recognition in *Who's Who Among America's Teachers*. She is a co-author of *Becoming the Professional Woman* in the PWN Library.

Contact:
Sharva Hampton-Campbell
P. O. Box 135
Champaign, IL 61824
(217) 202-5498
shamcamp@hotmail.com
www.protrain.net

TWENTY-TWO

TAKING PERSONAL INVENTORY

By Sharva Hampton-Campbell

It has already been established that this book is a necessary read for African-American women who are striving to be the best that they can be. In order to be our best, we have to come to terms with our past, live for today, and prepare for our future. One might ask, "How do I equip myself for this mighty task?" Well, this chapter was written to help you look within yourself and take personal inventory of your life so that you can "look back with more satisfaction and move forward with less distraction." Donna Summers wrote a song called "I Will Survive!" We have to affirm our survival. I created the following affirmation to help you grasp this concept.

In order to survive I must have **S**elf determination, **U**nderstand my purpose in life, **R**eward myself daily, **V**ivaciously pursue happiness, **I**ntegrate diet and exercise into my daily living, pursue a **V**ictorious relationship with God, and **E**levate my thinking.

"I will survive.... I know I'll stay alive... oh no not I, I will survive..... I will survive. Hey Hey."

Ponder this: Why is it important to affirm our survival? So much negativity has been drilled into us by others because of the way we look, speak, or even think. We can also be our own worst enemy with negative self-talk. We have to change this by replacing the negative with positive. For many years I have struggled with my weight and have yo-yo dieted, but nothing seemed to work until recently. While walking to my car, I looked up to God and said, "Lord why do we allow negativity to manifest itself into reality, but we brush off and become aloof to positive information. I have decided that I am going to speak positive about my weight from this day forward, and I ask that you allow my words to manifest in my spirit and become a reality. Let me begin now by thanking you for my 50 pounds of permanent weight loss." I speak this everyday and it is happening because I am well on my way. I would like you to create your own affirmation to help you let go of the negativity that is hold you back.

My affirmation:

_____

_____

Now take it a step further and connect it with a song, just as I did with "I Will Survive." By doing this activity, it is my hope that you will begin to appreciate yourself more. I would like you to say your affirmation and sing your song every morning when you wake-up, sing it throughout the day, and every night before you go to bed until you see the results you are looking for.

When I think about taking inventory, I am instantly reminded of when I worked for a well-known fast food chain as a Shift Leader. In this role, I assisted the Store Manger with counting all the product in the store and comparing it to the overall sales to make sure we were not wasting product and were making a profit. It required us to get up early in the morning and look deep within the stockpile of cups, plates, knives, forks, produce, frozen products, and canned goods. It was a tedious and somewhat grueling process; however, the end result provided us with information that helped the company develop ways to decrease waste, which in turn, led to a larger profit.

With this in mind, we are going to focus on the following areas: Your inner and outer self. Your inner self consists of your emotional and spiritual wellbeing, and your outer self consists of your physical wellbeing. These two areas make up the Mind Body and Spirit Connection.

You will need a journal to capture the true essence of the exercises in this chapter. Let's start by taking a minute to relax. We will use a technique called Diaphramic Breathing to collect ourselves. This type of breathing encompasses taking slow full breaths from your abdomen, instead of short shallow breaths from your chest.

Find a quiet place that is free from distractions. You can either sit in a chair with both feet on the floor, or lie down. Breathe in through your nostrils slowly while counting to four, hold your breath while you open your mouth, and breathe out through your mouth slowly while counting to four. Your stomach should be rising and falling with each breath, instead of your chest. If you become dizzy or light headed, decrease your counting to two or three. Place your hands on your thighs and close your eyes while conducting this exercise. Are you ready? Let's begin, inhale one, two, three four, pause, exhale, one two, three and four. Repeat this several times, or until your feel the tension leave your body and you begin to feel calm.

Get your journal and spend at least an hour answering the following questions:

1. Who am I?

2. What do I want out of life?

3. Where did I come from? (past)

4. Where am I now? (present)

5. Where am I going? (future)

Use the following page to jot down your thoughts if you don't have a journal.

_____

_____

_____

_____

_____

_____

_____

_____

_____

_____

_____

_____

Let's take a closer look at the **S.U.R.V.I.V.E.** Affirmation. The main components are Self-Determination, Purpose, Reward, Vivacious Pursuit, Integration, Victory and Elimination.

Self-Determination:

Self-determination is defined by The American Heritage dictionary as determination of one's own fate or course of action without compulsion; free will. The second principle of Nguzo Saba Kwanza, Kujichagulia (pronounced koo-jee-cha-goo-LEE-ah) states that self-determination is a pledge to define ourselves, name ourselves, create for ourselves, and speak for our selves, instead of allowing others to do this for us.

What does self-determination mean to you?

_____

_____

_____

George Kelly posted a statement on his website (www.allaboutgeroge.com) that read, "Self-determination acknowledges the possibility and hope of a new road, or a bridge that heals the past in order to compose a vibrant future."

How would you rate your level of self-determination?

POOR: I haven't overcome my past; therefore, I have no hope for the future.

FAIR: I'm working on overcoming my past and therefore, my future looks bright.

GOOD: My past made me stronger and equipped me to cross the bridge and head towards my destination.

Understand my PURPOSE in life:

The fifth principle of Kwanza is Nia (purpose) charges us to make our collective vocation the building and developing of our community, in order to restore our people to their traditional greatness. What is your greatness and how will you use it to build or develop your community? Initially, when I attempted to answer this question, I was baffled and my immediate response was, "I don't know." Then I thought, perhaps I need to spend some quiet time to reflect on this question. I would like you to do the same. Get your journal and find a quiet place where you won't be disturbed and spend 10 to 15 minutes clearing your mind. (Close your eyes and breath in slowly through your nostrils and out through your mouth until you feel your body relax.). Now collect your thoughts and answer the question. I have to warn you, this can be an emotional exercise. If you are truly honest with your feelings, you will more than likely become emotional, as you search for your true greatness (purpose in life). When I completed this exercise, I concluded that my purpose in life is to help others be the best that they can be mentally, physically and spiritually.

If you don't have a journal, you can use the following space to ponder your purpose.

_____

_____

_____

_____

REWARD yourself daily:

Reward yourself daily and celebrate! When you look at where you come from, where you are now, and where you are going, it's time to celebrate! Even if you believe your past, present and/or future looks bleak, search within and reflect on something positive, no matter how minute or miniscule it may seem. Use the following space to list your celebrations:

I celebrate the following:

Mine:	Yours:
Life	_____
The activity of my limbs	_____
A sound mind	_____
The ability to think for myself	_____

How have you rewarded yourself in the past? Rewards often time motivate you to continue your journey and rewards help build your self-esteem and confidence.

There are two types of rewards, external and internal, that motivate us to keep going. The external drive is often referred to as an extrinsic factor because it comes from the inside from material things, and acknowledgements from others, whereas, internal drives are called intrinsic because they come from the inside and are known as feelings and emotions.

VIVACIOUS pursuit of happiness:

When answering the following questions, be realistic and don't focus on material things or wealth. Look deep within.

What makes you happy?

_____

_____

_____

If you are not happy, what would make you happy?

_____

_____

_____

It makes me happy knowing that God loves me, and his unmerited favor has allowed me to live abundantly. My abundance has not come in the form of great wealth, but in giving me the tools to know my purpose in life and to fulfill my purpose.

INTEGRATION of diet and exercise in your daily living:

I can't say enough about the importance if eating right and exercising. Both are linked to living longer and disease-free. Research from the Harvard School of Public Health suggests the following:

— A diet rich in vegetables may prevent breast and prostate cancer.

— Colon cancer is more common among those who eat more red meat.

— High fat diets increase the risk of heart disease, strokes, and some types of cancer.

— A diet with too many carbohydrates increases the risk of obesity, diabetes, and heart disease.

Other health experts recommend incorporating whole grains, fresh fruits and vegetables, and at least eight 8-ounce glasses of water daily. Exercise is known to reduce anxiety and stress, improve your mood, sleep, and energy level. Controlling your weight prevents obesity.

Are you a health conscious person? _____

If so, how are you maintaining a healthy lifestyle?

_____

_____

_____

_____

_____

If you are not a health conscious person, what's holding you back?

_____

_____

_____

_____

_____

What are you going to do to alleviate these excuses?

_____

_____

_____

_____

_____

VIGOROUSLY pursue a relationship with God:

Who is He in your life and why is it important to have a relationship with Him?

_____

_____

_____

_____

_____

_____

I can't imagine living my life without being connected to God. I can talk to Him when I'm in trouble, and He listens without interruptions. He is not judgmental, but forgiving. His love is everlasting and I haven't found another who can provide me with this type of unconditional guarantee. When I was younger, I often wondered how I could develop a relationship with God. Over time, I learned that, by reading and studying His Holy Word, and living my life accordingly, our relationship would blossom.

What's your experience with getting to know God and getting closer to Him?

_____

_____

_____

_____

What would you life be without His presence?

_____

_____

_____

_____

_____

ELIMINATE negative thoughts:

Do you believe that negative thoughts affect who you are and your sense of purpose? It's true. The Bible says you are what you think (Proverb 23:7). If you allow negative thoughts to manifest, these thoughts can create havoc in your life.

Give three examples of situations that happened to you because of negative thinking.

My example: My day was ruined after I told myself that it would be. On that particular day, I overslept and was late to my first appointment. It seemed that Murphy's Law was present for the rest of the day.

Your examples:

1. _____

_____

_____

_____

2. _____

_____

_____

_____

3. _____

_____

_____

_____

    Please know that you have the power to reverse these thoughts. It's simple; learn to recognize when the negative thoughts start to enter your mind and "flip the script."

    For example, I could have easily turned my negative thought of "I'm going to have a horrible day because I'm already late" to "I'm excited about what today is going to bring. Even though I'm running late, I'm going to do my best to get back on schedule for the remainder of the day.

    If you consistently take a personal inventory of your thoughts and behaviors, you will be holding yourself accountable for change. You do have the power to change your thoughts and attitudes. May you be blessed on your journey to personal self-knowledge, growth, and empowerment.

Notes:

_____

_____

_____

_____

_____

_____

_____

_____

_____

_____

_____

_____

_____

_____

_____

_____

_____

_____

_____

_____

_____

_____

ABOUT THE AUTHOR

ALLISON DALRYMPLE, MSW, LCSW

Allison Dalrymple, founder & president of The International Institute for Self Discovery and Life Change, is a Licensed Clinical Social Worker with over fifteen years of experience in the field of social work. She has successfully worked with women affected by domestic violence, abuse, and rape; trauma victims, persons affected with mental health issues; disabled persons; the homeless; individuals with substance abuse issues; children and families; and persons in crisis.

Allison completed her Bachelors degree in Psychology and her Masters degree in Social Work at the University of Connecticut School of Social Work, in addition to a degree in Business Administration and Accounting.

The International Institute for Self Discovery and Life Change is a firm specializing in management consulting, training, human resources development, wellness-focused Employee Assistance Programs (EAP), workshops, seminars, consultation and coaching. Ms. Dalrymple's firm works with each client (individual, business or organization) to increase skills in goal achievement and employee work satisfaction.

Allison Dalrymple's areas of expertise include: executive, management and employee training; Employee Assistance Programs (EAP); Customer Service; Stress Management; Communication Seminars; Life Coach in Women's Wellness; Inspiration and Motivation; Women's Wellness; Welfare to Work; Career and Personal Enrichment; Trauma and Healing; Self-Esteem-Journey into Self Awareness; Second Phase of Life; and social work clinician supervision and exam coaching.

Contact:
The International Institute for Self Discovery and Life Change
P.O. Box 780
Manchester, CT 06045
(860) 647-6980
allisod22@aol.com
www.protrain.net

TWENTY-THREE

ABUSE NO MORE! HOW TO WALK AWAY FROM AN ABUSIVE RELATIONSHIP

By Allison Dalrymple, LCSW

*"I am on a difficult journey to a light at the end of the tunnel.
I know it will not be easy."*
— B.I., Woodbridge, VA.

Each year more than 2.5 million cases of battering are reported in the United States, and as many as 2,000 incidents of abuse turn into murder cases. Nearly 5.3 million intimate partner victimizations occur each year among U.S women ages 18 and older. This violence results in nearly 2 million injuries and nearly 1,300 deaths. According to a U.S Department of Justice report released in 2006, "intimate partner violence", referring to abuse between boyfriends and girlfriends as well as husbands and wives, affects about one in five women sometime in their lives.

No one is immune from domestic violence or an abusive relationship. It can happen to anyone at any time. It happens to men and women of all ages, from all cultures, across all socio-economic groups. Abuse knows no boundaries; it can happen to any of us. According to Jacquelyn Campbell, Ph.D., R.N., who has researched patterns of abuse for more than fifteen years and is currently a professor of nursing at John Hopkins University: "The only consistent risk factor for being abused is gender. That is, being a woman."

There is one factor that most experts agree will contribute to a woman's ending up in an abusive relationship. That factor is growing up with an abusive, violent father.

Spotting An Abusive Man

> *It is hard to realize that I am*
> *A worthwhile and capable person*
> *When I am not treated as such.*
> — W.L., Oklahoma City, OK

It's rare that a relationship starts out abusive, and in the beginning, abusive men are often charming—bringing flowers, calling frequently, buying gifts. Although an abusive man may seem romantic at first, his attentiveness soon turns to possessiveness, which in the end gives way to insults and violence. Many men who abuse women seem to share certain characteristics:

- They tend to be excessively jealous, which often is mistaken for love but has nothing to do with it.

- They tend to keep tabs on a victim, demanding to know her whereabouts every minute of the day.

- Often they are intensely committed, telling a woman such things as, "You're the only one who understands me," or "The world is so hard on a man like me," to make a woman feel guilty when she considers leaving him. Such statements are a form of control.

- Batterers also try to isolate their victims; the abuser cuts her off from family and friends by insisting they are against her. Abusive men blame others for their failings—his boss made him angry, or the world made him lose his temper.

- These men can also be sexually coercive; they may force a woman to do things she doesn't want to do, and even tamper with her birth control methods.

- Abusive relationships follow a pattern. After the violent display comes the calm, with profuse apologies and the promise of redemption. This "loving" period is always followed by more abuse. Angela Bassett, in the movie "What's Love Got To Do With It?", blamed herself after being beaten for not understanding her man enough. "It's been hard for him," she explained.

If your boyfriend or husband hits you once, it's rarely an isolated incident. When you decide to bring an end to an abusive relationship or situation, you must stick to your choice and be determined to end it. Have someone you trust help you end it, and make sure it ends. Pick up the telephone and call the National Domestic Violence Hotline at (800) 799-7233. It's important to talk to someone who understands what you're going through.

Breaking Free

> "Wisdom is knowing what to do next. Virtue is doing it."
> — David Starr Jordon

Overcoming abuse is a state of mind and a decision that goes with action. A woman above all, should keep safe and plan for the day she'll be ready to leave. In many situations, women are afraid to leave an abusive relationship. Fear can be paralyzing and debilitating, however it can also make you face reality. If you decide to leave an abusive relationship, you may not know whom to trust. Seeking help from what can be a racist and paternalistic law-enforcement and judicial system is especially unappealing to many black women. The message is, "Don't betray your community! Don't betray Black men!" This is a tremendous dilemma for many Black women.

As a community we must get across to our daughters, sisters and best friends, that while being in a relationship can be a wonderful and healthy thing, we cannot depend solely on others to define who we are and limit us.

Many African-American women believe they are superior to others around them if they are involved in a relationship with a man. This type of attitude leads many women to enter into abusive relationships. Women need to develop a sense of self-worth and focus on developing their skills. Many women use the " I got a man!" like a badge of honor for being in a relationship. (Too many of them believe that this somehow proves that they are better than a woman who doesn't have a male partner. It seems that even the brightest women can end up defining their value to society by whether or not she has a man). Whether you are a college grad, corporate executive, or homemaker, women need to put their faith into gaining the skills and knowledge they need to support themselves, rather than finding a good man.

In Terry McMillan's best selling novel *Waiting to Exhale*, Savannah's mother was willing to encourage her daughter to have an affair with a married man rather than remain alone. Thinking this way is dangerous for sisters. Many mentally or physically abusive relationships thrive on this low self-esteem mentality. Don't believe that it's better to be in an abusive relationship than to be alone. You need to value yourself first, and not based upon whether you are in a relationship with a man.

Abusive Relationship Safety Plan

If you find yourself in an abusive relationship, it may take you a while to realize that you need to get out. Eventually you will see that, no matter how often a man apologizes, he will strike you again! When you reach this stage, you will become more receptive to help. You will need to place yourself in a situation where you can see other women who are dealing with the same problems so you can figure out your options. You can find help in support groups and with counselors at local battered women's shelters (or call the National Domestic Violence toll free hot line 1-800-799-7233. For the hearing impaired, the toll free number is 1-800-787-3224). If you find yourself in the middle of a violent episode:

- Stay alert and try to keep something between you and the abuser.

- Stay out of the most dangerous rooms, such as the bathroom and kitchen.

- If your going to run out of the house, go to a safe destination like a convenience store, fire station, or anyplace where there are other people.

- Once you've decided to leave, be practical. Begin to pack small items such as photographs and leave them someplace where you can pick them up later. Put money away as well, either in a separate bank account or somewhere you know he won't find it.

- Most importantly, never boast about your plans to leave.

Signs Of Abuse

- When someone tells you that you must change who you are in order to conform to some ideal of his. By its very definition, love should make you feel better about yourself. It should add something special to what already exists. You should feel smarter, sexier and more capable. You should not feel like a student who has a lot to learn.

- A lover is a luxury, not a necessity. You were a whole person before you met this person. You are a whole person without him, and the presence of a lover should never make you feel less of a person.

- Don't confuse anxiety with love. It can never be right to change yourself in an unnatural way for a relationship. Trying to do this in the most intimate area of your life is self-betrayal.

- True romance is not based on fantasy. It's not unromantic to talk about what you really like or hate. Honesty is vital to true romance.

- Don't bend yourself out of shape to please your mate. If your partner continually implies that you're doing things wrong, then he has distracted you from asking the most important question in any relationship: "How does this man make me feel?"

- Don't become desperate to fix things in your relationship. Some men maybe critical by innuendo. Your husband points out that your friend Kate is always very well-dressed. "She takes real care of her appearance. That's why Dave is so proud of her." You feel more and more lost in the relationship, and become desperate to fix it. Occasionally, the feeling that you should be someone else arises at the very beginning of a relationship. After the first date, you find yourself feeling as though you're too shy, too exuberant, or too tall. You start apologizing to yourself or to him and try to fix things you never noticed before.

Healing And Recovery

Two people will never agree all the time. When they are able to discuss their differences, they often become better friends. When one person insists on always being in control, an abusive relationship can be the result. "Not everything that is faced can be changed." — Baldwin.

Very early in a relationship, we as women need to be very clear as to what we will and will not tolerate in a relationship, including being abused by:

- Revealing who we are very early in a relationship. If your new partner likes athletic women, don't lie and say you enjoy sports if you really hate them. The truth will come out eventually, and you will lead a life of misery, trying to be a jock when you aren't. Don't pretend even in a small way to fit into someone else's picture. Differences in a relationship are healthy, and if your new partner can't tolerate differences then perhaps you need to look elsewhere.

- Never accept your partner's withholding love until you make some change. Some criticism of you is valid. However, if you have to do something or change something about yourself in order to win his love, don't make a move. Protest the condition he is setting.

- Never start a guessing game about what you might be doing wrong. If your partner looks generally miserable in your company or isn't happy to see you, don't fall prey to scouring yourself for faults. There are people who make a practice of looking grim to get attention and get you to ask what's wrong. If he hasn't got the guts to tell you what's wrong, you shouldn't play the game of "Where Did I Fail?"

- Never trust that if you change in one way, he will love you again. The one-way fallacy is very common. If you change in his one way, there will always be something else. If he's giving you a hard time, discuss his behavior, not yours.

- Set an ultimatum if there is any physical abuse, and stick to it. Warn the person that one repetition is the end, and if that repetition occurs, you will go to any length to protect yourself from him. Remember: **violence escalates**!

- Beware of the trap that he's helpless, pathetic and had a difficult childhood. Women have been trained to be caretakers, and often this works to their disadvantage. Past suffering doesn't warrant present abuse. Don't make excuses for a person while you bend yourself out of shape to please him.

- Keep your friends. It's a very bad sign if your partner suddenly doesn't like people who have been close to you for a long time. He may be doing this subconsciously to strip you of allies. Don't let him do this to you.

- If you are in an unhappy relationship, start with a diary and see how many days per month you are really enjoying yourself and feel worthwhile. This is important because, if you're a person who twists yourself out of shape, you are very apt to delude yourself by saying, "I have to give ground this one time." There is a tendency to forget how much ground you have been giving over a period of time. It will give you perspective.

If you find yourself in an abusive relationship with no way out, the following daily affirmation can help you. Each day as you awake, touch your heart with your right hand and affirm:

- I am not to blame for being beaten and abused.

- I am not causing my partner's abusive behavior.

- I do not like being abused, and do not have to take it.

- I am a lovable, valuable human being.

- I can decide what is best for me.

- I can make changes in my life in order to be healthy and safe.

- I am a worthwhile person who can ask others for help.

- As a human being and as a partner, I have the right to be treated with respect and love.

Make it a point to repeat your affirmations as you do the dishes or fall asleep at night. Paste them on your visor and read them while you wait for the bus or traffic light to change.

May God bless you as you find fulfillment and purpose in your life!

Recommended Reading

What Causes Men's Violence Against Women? Editors Michele Harway. James M. O'Neil

Verbal Abuse Survivors Speak out on Relationship and Recovery by Patricia Evans

I Closed My Eyes. Revelations of a Battered Woman. Rebuilding Life after Domestic Violence by Michele Weldon

How to Stop Being Abused and How to Stop Abusing: The Emotionally Abusive Relationship by Beverly Engel

Why does He Do That? Inside the Minds of Angry and Controlling Men by Lundy Bancroft

Getting Free. You Can End Abuse and Take Back Your Life by Ginny NiCarthy, MSW

Notes:

ABOUT THE AUTHOR

CASSANDRA R. LEE

Mission: Education and Empowerment. Passion: Teaching through Speaking. These are the fuels to the existence of Cassandra "D.I.V.A. of Dialog™" Lee.

A certified trainer, national speaker, consultant, facilitator, and author, the "D.I.V.A. of Dialog™" is a messenger of soul-stirring and life-altering teachings.

In her interactive, theatrical seminars, she uses "divine inspiration vocally applied™" to educate the minds and stimulate the personal development of student and professional audiences nationwide on such topics as communication skills, financial empowerment, goal-achievement, health & wellness, leadership, professional development, and self-esteem.

Through her educational consulting firm SSANEE, Inc., Ms. Lee has presented for various organizations including the Woman2Woman Health & Beauty Expo, V103 Expo for Today's Black Woman, U.S. Department of Education, Social Security Administration, SkillPath Seminars, My Sister's Keeper Program, Jesse White Tumbling Team, Illinois Alliance of Boys and Girls Clubs, Hugh O'Brien Youth Leadership Program, Chicago Public Schools, Chicago Public Libraries, and many others.

Ms. Lee is a featured entrepreneur in *Who's Who in Black Chicago, the Inaugural Edition*. In addition, she is author of the audio CD *D.I.V.A.BITS™: 24 Enlightening Tips to Conquer Communication Skills* and co-author of *The Young Woman's Guide for Personal Success* in the PWN book library.

She is a member of the National Association for Campus Activities, Professional Woman Network, and Toastmasters International. She resides in Chicago, IL.

The "D.I.V.A. of Dialog™" is available to conduct a seminar, moderate a panel, facilitate a workshop, or present a speech at your next event.

Contact:
SSANEE, Inc.
P.O. Box 804546
Chicago, IL 60680
(773) 382-8721
SsaneeInc99@hotmail.com
www.ssanee.com
www.protrain.net

TWENTY-FOUR

EMBRACING
YOUR
AFROCENTRICITY

By Cassandra R. Lee

"...Making the decision to go natural has been a rite of passage, a ritual, a coming into one's own sense of place in an oftentimes hostile world that has frequently denied the Black woman her rightful place in the beauty spectrum." — Michael Cunningham,
Queens: Portraits of Black Women and Their Fabulous Hair

The year was 2003 and I had finally committed to doing something radically different with myself. It was a new season in my life and I was ready to break from the mode, ready to shake my known perceptions, ready to do something new. For most of my life I had become known as a woman who played it safe and rarely changed; a "comfort zone resident"; and a "plain Jane".

But by 2003, I had begun to live a new chapter in my professional life. I was no longer a full-time employee, but a full-time entrepreneur. I was living life as a risk-taker, generating my own income, and living out my goal of being an inspirational speaker. This professional change sparked within me an urging to make some changes in my personal life that reflected the connection I was feeling between my present and my future.

Thus, for my thirty-second birthday, I stopped playing it safe. I stepped out of my comfort zone. I took the risk I had been contemplating for months and radically changed my style. Yes, I did it! I cut the relaxer out of my hair and went "à la naturale". This was a bold and drastic leap for me. I felt highly liberated for breaking from my normal mode. I had lived my life under the persuasive power of the relaxer jar for over twenty years. I had spent much time searching for a healthy style, attempting to wear the "perfect" style, and struggling to maintain a versatile look that would reflect my inner being and my outer aspirations.

All of these frustrations went away with each snip of the scissors in June 2003. It was at this time that I boldly released the "wrap" and graciously welcomed "double-stranded twists", a new and natural hairstyle that allowed me to embrace my Afrocentricity.

A New Way Of Living

> *"If we don't change, we don't grow.*
> *If we don't grow, we aren't really living."* — Gail Sheehy

This chapter is written for you, the African-American woman who wants to experience a new way of living that connects you to your heritage and your aspirations. It is written for those of you who are struggling with the decision to go natural; battling with the disapproving stares you get each time you wear your Afrocentric apparel; and wrestling with the idea to change your Afrocentric look to fit in with the majority culture of your work environment.

In this chapter, I will provide you with information that will:

- Enlighten you on the *meaning* of Afrocentricity

- Identify the *barriers* to embracing your Afrocentricity; and

- Provide you with *strategies* to embrace your Afrocentricity.

In this chapter, we will tackle "Doubt" and "Naysayers", two primary barriers that discourage you from embracing your Afrocentricity. "Decide", "Claim Your Style", and "Love the New You" are three strategies that will coax you to commit to embrace your Afrocentricity. By the time you are done with this chapter, you will have a clear understanding of how to comfortably and confidently embrace your Afrocentricity.

I remember my introduction to the concept of Afrocentricity. I was an undergraduate at the University of Illinois in Urbana-Champaign. Back then, I thought to be Afrocentric meant that you had to change your birth name, wear black, green and red with Motherland medallions around your neck, and possess an attitude of defiance. Although this was how some of my classmates behaved, it was not a true depiction of being Afrocentric.

Later, through growth, education and insight, I learned that Afrocentricity requires that you have an awareness of your heritage, understanding of your spirituality, and a deep connection to your inner being that prompts you to take action to change your life for honest and prosperous living.

According to African Centered Education at Western Illinois University, "Afrocentricity is about the social, historical, cultural, and spiritual development of people of African decent. It is a way of looking at yourself differently from the way other people may see you... Afrocentricity helps you to better understand and appreciate who you are and how you can improve yourself. Afrocentricity is both old and new. That is to say, it celebrates our beautiful heritage and praises the best of our culture which we have today."

This viewpoint provides you with enlightenment on the meaning of Afrocentricity. It helps you to understand that embracing your Afrocentricity gives you a chance to live in today's society while weaving your historical heritage in subtle, conservative, or fashionable ways in various aspects of your life, such as:

- ☐ Books

- ☐ Clothes coloring

- ☐ Clothes fabric

- ☐ Clothes style

- ☐ Fragrances

- ☐ Hair styles

- ☐ Hobbies

- ☐ Home/office decorations

☐ Home/office furnishings

☐ Jewelry

☐ Music

☐ Shoes

☐ Travel

On your journey to embracing your Afrocentricity, you will discover what many sisters before you have found. It is easier to incorporate aspects of the Motherland into your personal style by focusing on your home furnishings, home decorations, jewelry, clothing, and hair. In your home, you can use art, throw pillows, pictures, rugs, masks, paints, and African artifacts to display your African heritage. In addition, you can use clothing and accessories to present your Afrocentric self to the world. Furthermore, you can use natural hairstyles such as Afros, twists, and locks to demonstrate your commitment to Afrocentricity.

In his book, *Queens: Portraits of Black Women and Their Fabulous Hair*, author Michael Cunningham states that, "Hair is so much more than just hair. Hair has the ability to unleash all of life's deepest emotions. Hair is about identity, beauty, racial pride, race politics, self-acceptance, self-expression, self-realization, class, status, fun, glamour, romance, fantasy, art, passion, joy, pain, freedom, enslavement, [and] power."

For me, hair was the simplest, yet most powerful place to start the transition into Afrocentric living.

Whether you decide to be Afrocentric in only your hairstyle or Afrocentric in everything that you do, this chapter will provide you with guidance on how to stay committed to embracing and expressing your heritage.

Barriers To Embracing Your Afrocentricity

Doubt

"How you view yourself, along with the beliefs you have about your
capabilities, will profoundly affect the results you produce."
— Zoie Kaye, **Saying 'No' to Negativity**

Do you find that you have tendencies of talking yourself out of wearing those cowrie shell earrings or that frizzy Afro because you "don't feel right"? Do you think at times that you will be better off keeping your curling iron than using beeswax? Are you contemplating staying with your beautician instead of finding a loctician? The most common barrier to embracing your Afrocentricity is the mindset you have toward your ability to live an Afrocentric existence.

There are times in your life when you doubt your ability to do certain things, and living day to day with an expressed level of heritage is no different. Keep in mind that doubt is the enemy to true expression. It is the main culprit to influencing you not to express your Afrocentricity. It makes you behave in a self-conscious manner. It causes you to waiver upon your decisions and falter in your actions. When you doubt yourself, you tend to "ride the fence", waste time, and regret your choices.

Therefore, don't let doubt get the best of you! Understand that embracing your Afrocentricity is a conscious thought that leads to conscious actions. Regardless of "feeling right", you must overcome doubt with actions. When you welcome the idea of adding heritage to your lifestyle, you will do the necessary things to make your heritage an intrinsic part of you.

Naysayers

"There is so much good in the worst of us,
And so much bad in the best of us,
That it ill behooves any of us,
To say anything about the rest of us." — Anonymous

Once you have squashed your internal dialogue, you must next deal with the external opinions of naysayers. According to *Merriam-Webster's Dictionary*, a naysayer is "one who denies, refuses, opposes, or is skeptical or cynical about something." Naysayers could be people you are close to, or they could be strangers. The opinions of naysayers are so powerful, that many of us find ourselves living our lives based on their criticisms of us. When embracing your Afrocentricity, understand that the philosophy of "not everything is for everybody" applies here. You will have relatives, friends, spouses, boyfriends, co-workers, and colleagues who will not think that you should change your current style to embrace the one of your ancestors. Some of them will say to you, "I don't think you will look right. I wouldn't do that if I were you." And you know what? They are not you!

I remember the day that I told my mom I was going to start wearing an Afro. Her response was, "You're gonna look funny with your hair like that." Actually, what was funny was her comment. It came seconds after she had described seeing one of my youngest sister's friends with a short, colored afro. My mom had described how cute the young lady looked and how the hairstyle complimented her face. After laughing off the shock of her statement, I inquired, "Oh, so I'm going to look funny, but she looks cute? Why can't I be cute no matter what since

I'm your daughter?" Then I laughed again. This was done to keep me from internalizing the weight of her words. Also, it was done to keep me from being slapped down by my mom, just in case she thought I was being "a smart mouth" with her. After my mom, my two sisters, and I had a good laugh, my mom realized the irony of her statement and agreed that I, too, would look nice with my hair in a short, colored Afro.

On that day, I learned a valuable lesson: I must be prepared for the perceptions of naysayers.

Even though my mom had not intended to be skeptical and cynical about my decision to go natural, her response immediately turned her into a naysayer because of her perception toward natural hairstyles. My mom perceived the colored Afro to be a fad that young people were doing these days to be different. Her sentiment was that someone my age should wear a more conservative hairstyle. Once I understood her perception, I was able to respond to her opposition in a confident way. You must learn to do the same.

Exercise
"Know Your Naysayers"
In the exercise below, determine who the naysayers are in your life. Determine the perceptions they have toward Afrocentricity. Decide your response that can weaken their perception.

EXAMPLE:
Naysayer: Mom

Their Perception: Natural hairstyles are for the younger generations

My Response: All women like hairstyles that make them feel and look good

Naysayer: _____

Their Perception: _____
_____

My Response:_____
_____

Naysayer: _____

Their Perception: _____
_____

My Response:_____
_____

Naysayer: _____

Their Perception: _____
_____

My Response:_____
_____

Naysayer: _____

Their Perception: _____
_____

My Response:_____
_____

Naysayers can stifle your motivation. Their perceptions can limit their understanding of your decision. Their lack of encouragement can deter you from fulfilling your vision. Their lack of support can shatter your confidence.

The best way to deal with naysayers is to first be unwavering in your confidence to change your style to reflect your Afrocentricity. Next, prepare yourself with responses that will weaken their perceptions regarding you becoming Afrocentric. Finally, use their criticisms as fuel to stand firm on embracing your Afrocentricity.

Strategies To Embracing Your Afrocentricity

I Decide

"Once you make a decision, the universe conspires to make it happen."
— Ralph Waldo Emerson

Sure you can talk it over with your mother, discuss it with your best friend, or hash it through with your husband; however, the bottom line is that YOU must make the decision to live your life with a new and different style. Stop procrastinating! Get rid of your doubts! From this moment forward, decide to embrace your heritage.

I, _____,
have made the decision to change my style to embrace my Afrocentricity.
On this day _____, 200_____.

Claim Your Style

"Whenever you find yourself on the side of the majority,
it's time to pause and reflect." — Mark Twain

Once you decide that you will embrace your Afrocentricity, you must understand who you are at your core. This insight will give you clarity on how to use Afrocentric flair to complement your natural style.

Style is an essential element to your existence. As stated in the *Merriam-Webster Dictionary,* "It is a distinctive manner of expression or custom of conducting yourself."

Here are four **"CATEGORIES OF AFROCENTRICITY"**. Determine the category that best describes you:

- **"CASUAL NATURAL"**: Women in this category have a simplistic way of adding Afrocentricity to their lives. They wear a short, natural hair cut, twists, or dreadlocks, along with minimal or cowrie shell jewelry, and little or no makeup.

- **"CHIC SOPHISTICATED"**: Women in this category maintain professional, classic attire sprinkled with natural hairstyles and conservative jewelry, usually silver.

- **"AFRO GLAM"**: Women in this category exhibit Afrocentric flair with colors, jewelry, fabrics, and hairstyles that makes the Afrocentricity sparkle, gleam, and shout.

- **"AUTHENTICALLY AFROCENTRIC"**: Women in this category have a style that is completely Afrocentric from inside out. Every aspect of her including spirit, clothing, eating habits, and home, encapsulates the essence of the Motherland.

These four categories help you to determine your "distinctive manner of expression". This insight helps you to determine your core style so that you may comfortably embrace your Afrocentricity.

Another way to establish your core style is to think about the image you portray to the world when you are:

Exercise: "My Core Style Image"

- At work_____

- At play _____

- Handling business_____

- In relationships _____

- With family and friends _____

One final measure that you can take is to determine the characteristics of your core style by asking yourself "What five (5) words describe who I am the majority of the time in all aspects of my life?" Some choices are:

EXERCISE: "Characteristics of My Core Style"

Aggressive	Elegant	Powerful
Articulate	Energetic	Professional
Assertive	Experienced	Relaxed
Attractive	Flexible	Reliable
Capable	Friendly	Responsible
Casual	Happy	Sassy
Compassionate	Honest	Sensual
Conservative	Intelligent	Sexy
Cooperative	Knowledgeable	Sophisticated
Creative	Passive	Unconventional
Detailed	Plain	Well-groomed

When I embraced my Afrocentricity in 2003, I discovered that I am "Chic Sophisticated" and my core style is a "sexy, sensual, sophisticated, sassy, 'Sistah-gurl'". I realized that these are the consistent characteristics that I portray the majority of the time in all aspects of my life, whether I am at work, at play, handling business, in relationships, or with family and friends.

My natural mannerisms, speaking style, body shape, body posture, eyes, and attitude reflect the "sophisticated, sensual, sexy, and 'Sistah-gurl'" aspects of me. I use clothing, jewelry, and hairstyles with Afrocentric flair to represent the "sassy" aspect of me.

How about you? What is the image that you portray to the world? What "Category of Afrocentricity" do you fit? Which characteristics can you use to bring forth your Afrocentric nature? Take a few minutes to review each section to determine your natural style.

Use the results from each category to help you claim your style. Claiming your style will ease the burden of weaving Afrocentric elements into your daily living.

Love The New You

"I prefer to be true to myself, even at the hazard of incurring the ridicule of others, rather than to be false, and to incur my own abhorrence."
— Frederick Douglass

Making the decision to enhance your life in Afrocentric ways and taking the steps to claim your Afrocentric style must be accompanied by the commitment to love the new you.

This is a new journey for you and there will be challenging times ahead. When you feel that you can't stay committed, or when the doubt becomes unbearable, use the following prescription to remain faithful and consistent in loving the new you:

Exercise: "Self-Love Prescription"
- Smile at yourself in the mirror; 3 times a day, 7 days a week

- State one compliment out loud regarding your looks; once a day, 7 days a week

- Pamper your new areas of Afrocentricity; once a week; 4 times a month

- Enhance your Afrocentricity with only items that compliment your new style; once every 3 months

When you love the new you, it becomes a spiritual transformation that seeps through your pores into all that you do. You become connected to your inner-self, and this generates an underlying energy that people see and feel, causing them to comment on the change and compliment you on your radiant beauty.

Afrocentricity is a school of thought that has been embraced by many African-Americans, male and female, young and old, for years. It's a way of living that reminds us that we are descendants of Kings and Queens. It's an awareness that provides us with a strong sense of pride and a healthy level of self-esteem. Whether you made a conscious choice for spiritual reasons or a conscious choice for fashionable reasons, embracing your Afrocentricity is a choice that empowers you to take risks and challenges you to live a spiritually enriched life.

Congratulations on your change!

Recommended Reading

Books

Becoming the Professional Woman edited by Linda Ellis Eastman

I Can See You Naked by Ron Hoff

Queens: Portraits of Black Women and Their Fabulous Hair by Michael Cunningham and George Alexander

Saying 'No' to Negativity by Zoie Kaye

Self-Esteem & Empowerment for Women edited by Linda Ellis Eastman

Magazines

Black Enterprise

Ebony

Essence

Websites

http://pages.prodigy.net/gmoses/moweb/unity.htm

www.dimensionsnews.com/feb6Afrocentricity.htm

www.eleganceinstyle.com

www.inspiredlocs.com

www.m-w.com/dictionary

www.nappturality.com

www.quoteland.com

www.wiu.edu/users/mutkh3/ace/afro.htm

Notes:

_____

_____

_____

_____

_____

_____

_____

_____

_____

_____

_____

_____

_____

_____

_____

_____

_____

_____

_____

_____

_____

ABOUT THE AUTHOR

CLAUDIA WHITE

Born on the west side of Chicago, Claudia White graduated from Purdue University with a BS in Business and minors in Marketing and Psychology. Her extensive career as a sales representative began with American Hospital Supply. She then broke into the field of advertising with the Leo Burnett advertising agency in Chicago, IL. After Leo Burnett, Claudia White became a Marketing Communications Specialist for General Electric Medical Systems in Milwaukee, WI. Claudia then joined Bristol-Myers Squibb in the Princeton, NJ headquarters as a Marketing Communications Manager. In this role, Claudia was responsible for placing, originating, and evaluating print advertising and visual media advertising for ostomy, wound care, and specialty product lines. She is currently a Senior Hospital Sales Specialists for King Pharmaceuticals in the Columbus Ohio market. There, she is charged with penetrating teaching hospitals in the Columbus area, and orchestrating/executing sales agendas for multi-million surgical and infectious disease products lines. She gives thanks to her niece Whitney Clair White, an undergraduate at Northwestern University for contributing to this project.

Contact:
Positive Pathways Unlimited
1209 Hill Road North #249
Pickerington, OH 43147
(614) 570-2057
Wcdub11@aol.com
www.protrain.net

TWENTY-FIVE

DARE TO DREAM: THINKING OUTSIDE THE BOX

By Claudia White

What is a dream? What does it mean *to* dream? Perhaps the more important question is how does one go about achieving a dream. A dream is often an intangible thing. Illusive and fantastical, dreams are visions that motivate and inspire us. Often when burdened by obstacles our dreams slip from our grasp. Even so, I have come to believe that thinking outside the box has enabled me to overcome many obstacles that have stood in the way of my dreams, and I think that if you allow yourself to honestly reflect on what your dreams are, and who you are, thinking outside the box can help you get closer to your dreams. While reading my story, my past challenges and future aspirations, consider your own situation. Write your dreams down. Consider which dreams seem most attainable. Which dreams are most important? In this chapter, with my story, and the stories of those who have inspired me, I hope to encourage and inspire you to allow the power of thinking outside the box to transform your life.

But what is this phrase "thinking outside the box"? And who am I to instruct you on how to achieve your dreams? The first question can be more readily dealt with. Thinking outside the box is a phrase we often hear in the work place or commercials; a characterless expression a boss tells you to increase productivity. I, however, believe that thinking outside the box is more than a useless phrase. To think outside the box is to reform the very way you see the world. It is to make ready and flexible an ability to shift ones very own paradigm. It calls upon your ability to think in metaphors. In order to think outside the box one must maintain identity while adapting to difficult situations that present themselves.

Given my interpretation of the phrase, I want you to know who "I" am. I am a black, successful business woman. I am a Chicagoan and a person who refuses to quit. I am a woman who doesn't take herself too seriously; a woman not afraid to have a good laugh or cry whenever I need to. I am an eternal optimist, comfortable in all environments whether lounging with friends or closing a multimillion dollar deal. But most importantly I am a person who believes in God. It is necessary to take a look at yourself the way I have, in order to think outside the box. How would you describe yourself? What could you change about yourself? Identify your resources, strengths and weaknesses and write them down. By evaluating myself in such a way, I have been able to understand my weaknesses and turn them into strengths.

As a child growing up in the projects on the west side of Chicago, the possibilities for a bright future were bleak. Like others, I did not live in the projects by choice; rather I was there by circumstance. The schools I attended only added to my sense of hopelessness; I felt I would never make it out of the ghetto. Which childhood experiences are standing in the way of your dreams? If you experienced points of hopelessness, how did you overcome them? Your methods then may help you now. In my situation and despite the effects of my surroundings, I still harbored bigger dreams. Even though the threat of being teased forced me to keep my dreams a secret, my mother remained aware of my aspirations. She saw my true potential and encouraged me to be the best I could be.

My mother's guiding light and encouragement constantly manifested itself in my imagination. Playtime became a time for me to explore my talents. Every time I played with girlfriends or by myself, I became a business woman. Not *a* business woman, rather I became "*the*" business woman. With the help of my mother's old purse I even had a briefcase for the part. This reoccurring child's play was not a coincidence. When you think back, was there a particular game or role that you often played? Your past enjoyments could direct you on your future path. The role of "the business woman" that I repeatedly took on was indeed a sign for the future; one of God's purposes for me on this planet.

Unfortunately, no one remains a child forever. When we 'mature' the light of imagination once possessed is dimmed by the realities of the world. By the time I was in high school, my dream of becoming a successful business woman had all but vanished. Not only had I lost faith, but I was surrounded by people who were neither encouraging, nor exhibiting dreams of their own. My counselors and peers certainly did not consider college as an option for me. Less than 20% of my senior graduating class of several hundred students went on to any type of school of higher learning. Therefore, after high school, with economic pressure rearing its head, I sought employment.

As a receptionist, I found work with The Continental Bank located in downtown Chicago. It was not challenging, but it provided a source of income. Today, I am thankful that I found that job because employment forced my state of mind to mature. I got into the habit of having a schedule and responsibilities. With that job, I was thrust into an environment with black business women who walked and talked the way I wanted to. I was reborn as the living symbols of success fostered a new strength within.

This inner strength became visible to those around me. My boss recognized it, and told me I would make an excellent candidate for attending the American Institute of Banking. After briefly attending the institute I knew college was the next step toward my dream. I could not allow bad grades or a lack of money to stop me. There was a point when I consciously decided that my dreams were worth striving for. Which obstacles from your past have lingered and inhibited you today? What can be done now to overcome those obstacles? Ask yourself, what are your dreams worth?

Getting into Purdue University took hard work, writing, applying for financial aid, and taking the SAT's were tasks I had to push myself to accomplish. Still, a year from the date I began working at the large bank in Chicago, I was accepted into Purdue. I graduated four years later with a BS degree in Business with minors in Marketing and Psychology. Yes, I graduated and am currently a senior hospital sales specialist for a pharmaceutical company headquartered in Princeton, NJ. But this does not mean that the barriers have stopped coming;

thinking outside the box has allowed me to work beyond problems of my past and towards a better future.

To ensure that I never stop dreaming, I have called upon inspirational black female figures that have also gotten to where they are by thinking outside of the box. Some of these women are famous while others are my closest friends. Despite their differences they are connected in their persistence and belief in their ability to attain their dreams.

Maya Angelo is not an unfamiliar name (and if she is unfamiliar to you, then I advise you to seek her literature); I have found her writing and persona to be of strength and persistence, as she consistently challenges norms and evaluates the meaning of success. She states, "Don't make money your goal. Instead pursue the things you love doing, and do them so well that people can't take their eyes off of you. All other tangible rewards will come as a result," (Cain, Joy Duckett. Gregory, Deborah. Johnson, Pamela. Robotham, Rosemarie. *Essence Special Collectors Edition*. Ed. Hinds, Patricia M. 2002 Essence Communications Partners and Time Inc Home Entertainment). This quote is significant to me, as it highlights the importance of seeing past standards. Many people pursue professions because of money. Instead, Maya Angelo encourages you to designate the things you love as your goals, to think outside the box and see past the lure of doing things strictly for greed.

Adanech Spratlin is another female that inspires me. Her story may be less familiar than that of Maya Angelo, but Adanech is overcoming obstacles in her life by thinking outside the box and seeing past her physical limitations. I first heard her story on Oprah, and read about it later in the *Atlanta Journal*. Adanech was born in a poor suburb in Ethiopia. Abandoned by her mother, Adanech was being raised by her elderly grandmother when she was victim of an accident. On the way home from the store, Adanech was hit by a train while crossing a set of railroad tracks. The train severed her right arm and crushed her right leg. Yonas Kebede, a children's aid worker, met this little girl in a hospital in Ethiopia. Being so touched by her spirit, he arranged to bring her to America. He not only had Adanech fitted with a prosthetic leg, but introduced her to her future adoptive family, the Spratlins. ("An Inspiration, stroke by stroke". *Atlanta Journal- Constitution* 2004) Adanech had to quickly learn how to fit into her new culture and to speak English.

But her amazing story does not end there. Upon seeing her new brothers swimming in their family pool, and competing in swimming matches in their local schools, Adanech began teaching herself how to swim with just one arm and one leg. Despite being a double amputee Adanech was determined to be an athlete. Now Adanech faces the possibility of competing in the 2008 Paralympic games in Beijing.

The story of this little girl reinforces the power of attaining one's goals by means of thinking outside the box. If she had catered to the finite limitations of being a "handicap" then her dream of being an athlete would never have been realized. Thus Adanech demonstrates the importance of stomping out obstacles by shifting your paradigm. You may not be adopted nor have a prosthetic limb, but all human beings have some limitation that can impede progress. These limitations may be physical, mental or environmental, but they can still be overcome if you persevere.

I would like to offer another story of a woman overcoming obstacles in her life. Betty Jackson is Executive VP/Chief Operating Officer for a social service agency that works with disabled Chicagoans. She, too, is a successful Black businesswoman. However, the obstacle she has had to overcome has been her problems with weight.

Betty had been morbidly obese for most of her life. Like many of us, Betty tried a myriad of diets without any lasting results. As Betty experienced the passing of her mother, sister, close girlfriend and significant other due to diseases and medical conditions that were out of their control, Betty realized she needed to take control of her life. It became clear to Betty that she did not want to prematurely die of a health problem that was potentially in her control. She thus took action and found an excellent personal trainer in my sister, Michelle White, and has come to love exercise; "It affects my entire state of mind, body and spirit. I'm learning not to be as much of an emotional eater anymore."(Jackson, Betty Executive VP, Chief Operating Officer, December, 2004). Betty was able to change her perception of herself and reality; she transformed her life by seeing past the limitations of obesity. She has since lost 180 lbs, and with each pound her dream moves closer to reality.

The last story I would like to offer to demonstrate the power of thinking outside the box is that of a close friend of mine. Geraldine Mason is an African-American woman and single parent of three who is currently a full-time student at Ohio State University, and hair stylist in Columbus, OH. When asked to contribute to this book, I knew right away that I had to share her story for it truly demonstrates what can be overcome if one is able to see past the limitations of their given circumstance. Like many of us, Geraldine is working to overcome the negativity in her past.

As she matured, Geraldine was continuously deterred from her dreams. "You can't do it Geraldine! You're not smart enough Geraldine! You're not pretty enough! You cannot have this". For a while Geraldine allowed outside forces to hinder her. She began to believe that she was inferior to her siblings and to the rest of the world. But there came a point, like there has for myself and for many of you, when the walls of the box that was her life began to close in. No one can live in a box forever, without room to breathe and grow. There was thus only one thing for Geraldine to do, and that was to break through that box. There existed a true potential Geraldine felt within herself that allowed her to invest in her future. Is there any aspect of Geraldine's story that translates to your life? It is important that you believe in your own true potential as Geraldine did. Ask yourself whether you have faith in your own abilities. If not, then what can you do to build a belief and strength within yourself?

These stories like my own have a commonality. In each story, the person realized at some point that their way of life was insufficient. Upon the acknowledgement of their dissatisfaction with reality they called upon an ability to see past the roles given to them. It is difficult to make the leap between realizing a dream and achieving it. This I will not sugar coat. But I encourage you to sit down and make a personal inquiry as to what your true passions and talents are.

The first insight I have on achieving dreams can be seen in the story of my youth. There is an indistinguishable power children possess. They are able to see past the complications of their existence simply with the power of "imagination". By de-establishing reality, reforming and molding it with their imaginations, children are able to think outside of the box. Therefore, call upon the things that inspired you as a child.

Identify what it is you want. This can be difficult as it is almost impossible to be honest with oneself. To distinguish what it is you really want from what is easily attainable can be incomprehensible for the mind at first, but temporary satisfaction versus fulfillment of a dream will make a world of difference.

Surrounding yourself with positive people eases the difficulty of realizing what it is you really want. We all have people in our lives that we consider to be our best friends. Nevertheless, take an inventory of these "friends" and ask yourself if they are helping you to sink or to swim. I am not encouraging you to abandon those who have been there for you in the past just because they are not helping you now, but be aware of "dead weights" so to speak. Try sharing your ideas and aspirations with your friends and observe their reaction. Did they laugh at your ideas? Did they attempt to convince you that there's no way "someone like you" could attain that goal? Or were they inspired and supportive? Instead of spending time with those who do not believe in you, find role models in your life that you can immolate. There is nothing wrong with having certain celebrities as role models, but there can be no direct contact between you and a famous person. You can't call a celebrity at night when you are in need. You can't go to church and worship together. Once you do find a role model that can be in your life, keep in mind what qualities they possess that inspire you to be more like them.

As I stated above, I greatly admire Maya Angelo. I like the way she carries herself with dignity and grace. My goal then is not to become her, but rather to incorporate the qualities of hers which I have a high regard for into my life. Remember, that this dream is about you. Take excellent care of yourself and do whatever it takes to build your self-confidence. Role models are beneficial, but when the cookie crumbles the only person who can help you is yourself.

When you feel burdened, discouraged, or if the dream appears to be unachievable I recommend that you that you "free your mind". I found a quote in the *LA Times* that describes little things someone can do to free their mind. "Monotonous routine breeds monotonous thinking. Dare to escape from your mundane habits. Sleep on the other side of the bed. Take a new route to work. Sign up for courses outside your field. Journey to a neighborhood you've never visited. Jolt your mind from its workaday trance by taking short, daily "field trips away from your workplace," (Vaughn, Susan. "Ways to free up your brain". LA Times. Monday, January 11, 1999). This will not only help you to keep your sanity, but it will also help you to stay positive and focused on what you need to do.

In conclusion, determine for yourself what is realistic and achievable. Going after what you want is no safe endeavor. But if you create a strategy and are not afraid to put yourself on the line for what you believe in, you will be satisfied. What was done yesterday, last week or last year has nothing to do with what's going on in your life right now. Never feel that it is too late to achieve your dream. You must work at bettering yourself, being stronger and more persistent. Work each year to achieve your hopes and desires. Next year, God willing, I will be turning fifty, an age that until recently has been identified as "old". But I will not let age hinder me; I will continue to see past the stereotypes that have been set for those over fifty.

In pursuing my dreams I have been transformed by thinking outside the box. It has helped me understand that I don't ever have to give up. Living this way combined with my faith in God has guided me on the right path. I will continue to ask for His guidance, and pray that He gives me strength. My hope for you, the reader, is that you will let nothing stand in the way of your dreams. Every time you come upon an obstacle, just use your imagination and think outside the box. You shall prevail. If there is one thing that you take away from this chapter, given my story, and the stories of those inspirational females, then I hope it is the power of a belief in oneself. Society may tell you that

Black women can't do it. People around you may tell you that *you* can't do it but do not be afraid to dream; dare to dream.

Dream worksheet:

1. What are your current dreams?_____

_____

_____

2. Write your dreams down. Prioritize them. _____

_____

_____

3. What did you dream about as a child? _____

_____

_____

4. Thinking back to the one game and/or role you loved playing as a child, who did you pretend to be (i.e., For me, it was a business woman. Who was it for you? A doctor/nurse, teacher, musician, model?) _____

_____

_____

5. What is stepped in the way of you achieving those childhood dreams? _____

_____

_____

6. What's stopping you from achieving those childhood dreams now that you're an adult?_____

_____

_____

7. Is there any part of your life now that resembles your childhood games?_____

_____

_____

8. Are these realistic dreams for you to achieve in your lifetime?_____

_____

_____

9. If so, what's keeping you from fulfilling these dreams? _____

_____

_____

10. What sacrifices are you willing to make to accomplish your dreams? _____

_____

_____

Recommended Reading

Awaken The Giant Within by Anthony Robbins

Attitude is Everything by Keith Harrell

Who Moved my Cheese by Spencer Johnson, MD

The Seven Habits of Highly Effective People by Stephen Covey

The Game of Life and How to Play It by Florence Scovel Shinn

The Purpose Driven Life by Rick Warren

Notes:

_____

_____

_____

_____

_____

_____

_____

_____

_____

_____

_____

_____

_____

_____

_____

_____

_____

_____

_____

_____

THE PROFESSIONAL WOMAN NETWORK
Training and Certification on Women's Issues

Linda Ellis Eastman, President & CEO of The Professional Woman Network, has trained and certified over one thousand individuals to start their own consulting/seminar business. Women from such countries as Brazil, Argentina, the Bahamas, Costa Rica, Bermuda, Nigeria, South Africa, Malaysia, and Mexico have attended trainings.

Topics for certification include:
• Diversity & Multiculturalism
• Women's Issues
• Women: A Journey to Wellness
• Save Our Youth
• Teen Image & Social Etiquette
• Leadership & Empowerment Skills for Youth
• Customer Service & Professionalism
• Marketing a Consulting Practice
• Professional Coaching
• Professional Presentation Skills

If you are interested in learning more about becoming certified or about starting your own consulting/seminar business contact:

The Professional Woman Network
P.O. Box 333
Prospect, KY 40059
(502) 566-9900
lindaeastman@prodigy.net
www.prowoman.net

The Professional Woman Network
Book Series

Becoming the Professional Woman
Customer Service & Professionalism for Women
Self-Esteem & Empowerment for Women
The Young Woman's Guide for Personal Success
The Christian Woman's Guide for Personal Success
Survival Skills for the African-American Woman

Forthcoming Books:
Overcoming the SuperWoman Syndrome
You're on Stage! Image, Etiquette, Branding & Style
Women's journey to Wellness: Mind, Body & Spirit
A Woman's Survival Guide for Obstacles, Transition & Change
Women a Leaders: Strategies for Empowerment & Communication
Beyond the Body: Developing Inner Beauty
The Young Man's Guide for Personal Success
Emotional Wellness for Women Volume I
Emotional Wellness for Women Volume II
Emotional Wellness for Women Volume III

These books will be available from the individual contributors, the publisher (www.prowoman.net), Amazon.com, and your local bookstore.